Endangered
Animals

VOLUME 3

Boa, Jamaican – **Danio,** Barred

GROLIER
EDUCATIONAL

Published 2002 by Grolier Educational, Danbury, CT 06816

This edition published exclusively for the school and library market

Produced by Andromeda Oxford Limited
11–13 The Vineyard, Abingdon,
Oxon OX14 3PX, U.K.
www.andromeda.co.uk

Principal Contributors: *Amy-Jane Beer, Andrew Campbell, Robert and Valerie Davies, John Dawes, Jonathan Elphick, Tim Halliday, Pat Morris. Further contributions by David Capper and John Woodward*

Project Director: *Graham Bateman*
Managing Editors: *Shaun Barrington, Jo Newson*
Editor: *Penelope Mathias*
Art Editor and Designer: *Steve McCurdy*
Cartographic Editor: *Tim Williams*
Editorial Assistant: *Marian Dreier*
Picture Manager: *Claire Turner*
Production: *Clive Sparling*
Indexers: *Indexing Specialists, Hove, East Sussex*

Reproduction by A. T. Color, Milan
Printing by H & Y Printing Ltd., Hong Kong

Set ISBN 0-7172-5584-0

Library of Congress Cataloging-in-Publication Data

Endangered animals.
     p. cm.
       Contents: v. 1. What is an endangered animal? -- v. 2. Addax - blackbuck -- v. 3. Boa, Jamaican - danio, barred -- v. 4. Darter, Watercress - frog, gastric brooding -- v. 5. Frog, green and golden bell - kestrel, lesser -- v. 6. Kestrel, Mauritius - Mulgara -- v. 7. Murrelet, Japanese - Pupfish, Devil's Hole -- v. 8. Pygmy-possum, mountain - Siskin, red -- v. 9. Skink, pygmy blue-tongued - tragopan, Temminck's -- v. 10. Tree-kangaroo, Goodfellow's - zebra, mountain.
    ISBN 0-7172-5584-0 (set : alk. paper) -- ISBN 0-7172-5585-9 (v. 1 : alk. paper) – ISBN 0-7172-5586-7 (v. 2 : alk. paper) -- ISBN 0-7172-5587-5 (v. 3 : alk. paper) – ISBN 0-7172-5588-3 (v. 4 : alk. paper) -- ISBN 0-7172-5589-1 (v. 5 : alk. paper) – ISBN 0-7172-5590-5 (v. 6 : alk. paper) -- ISBN 0-7172-5591-3 (v. 7 : alk. paper) – ISBN 0-7172-5592-1 (v. 8 : alk. paper) -- ISBN 0-7172-5593-X (v. 9 : alk. paper) – ISBN 0-7172-5594-8 (v. 10 : alk. paper)
    1. Endangered species--Juvenile literature. [1. Endangered species.] I. Grolier Educational (Firm)

QL83 .E54 2001
333.95'42--dc21

00-069134

Contents

About This Set

Endangered Animals is a 10-volume set that highlights and explains the threats to animal species across the world. Habitat loss is one major threat; another is the introduction of species into areas where they do not normally live.

Examples of different animals facing a range of problems have been chosen to include all the major animal groups. Fish, reptiles, amphibians, and insects and invertebrates are included as well as mammals and birds. Some species may have very large populations, but they nevertheless face problems. Some are already extinct.

Volume 1—What Is an Endangered Animal?—explains how scientists classify animals, the reasons why they are endangered, and what conservationists are doing about it. Cross-references in the text (volume number followed by page number) show relevant pages in the set.

Volumes 2 to 10 contain individual species entries arranged in alphabetical order. Each entry is a double-page spread with a data panel summarizing key facts and a locator map showing its range.

Look for a particular species by its common name, listed in alphabetical order on the Contents page of each book. (Page references for both common and scientific names are in the full set index at the back of each book.) When you have found the species that interests you, you can find related entries by looking first in the data panel. If an animal listed under Related endangered species has an asterisk (*) next to its name, it has its own separate entry. You can also check the cross-references at the bottom of the left-hand page, which refer to entries in other volumes. (For example, "Finch, Gouldian **4:** 74" means that the two-page entry about the Gouldian finch starts on page 74 of Volume 4.) The cross-reference is usually made to an animal that is in the same genus or family as the species you are reading about; but a species may appear here because it is from the same part of the world or faces the same threats.

Each book ends with a glossary of terms, lists of useful publications and websites, and a full set index.

Boa, Jamaican

Epicrates subflavus

Native only to Jamaica, the Jamaican boa—known locally as "yellowsnake"—has suffered from habitat destruction, predation, and deliberate killing. It is now difficult to find in many parts of its former haunts, but sizable captive populations exist in the United States and Europe.

The genus *Epicrates,* to which the Jamaican boa belongs, contains 10 species, one of which lives in South America. The other nine are distributed throughout the West Indies. They are all nonvenomous, using constriction to kill their prey. Although they are harmless, they are, like many snakes, often killed out of fear.

The present distribution of the Jamaican boa is patchy as a result of habitat fragmentation and destruction over the years. During the period of European settlement in Jamaica, which began with the Spanish in the 15th century, land was increasingly cleared for agriculture. Farmers brought in pigs, goats, cats, and dogs, and they attracted rats. Mongoose were introduced to control rats, and they started preying on the native fauna, particularly young snakes.

Agriculture is the main source of income in Jamaica, but there is also bauxite mining and tourism, both of which encroach on the boa's natural habitat. There are still some fairly remote, forested areas where the boa thrives, but more roads are being built into the forest, giving easier access to subsistence farmers, woodcutters, charcoal burners, and hunters. Charcoal burning is particularly destructive to the boa's habitat—large amounts of timber are needed to produce a relatively small amount of charcoal.

The Jamaican boa is not in immediate danger of extinction in its main areas, but small, localized populations are at risk. Exactly how many Jamaican boas remain outside captivity is hard to estimate; the boa is difficult to spot in the wild, preferring quiet

DATA PANEL

Jamaican boa

Epicrates subflavus

Family: Boidae

World population: Unknown

Distribution: Jamaica

Habitat: Mainly forests on honeycomb limestone, although it can be found in moist, tropical forest areas. Safest population in the Blue Mountains in Portland, eastern Jamaica, and the Cockpit Country in Trelawny, northern Jamaica. It is adaptable and has been found in coconut and banana plantations, often near houses

Size: Length: 6–8 ft (1.8–2.4 m)

Form: Long, slender snake with a broad head; anterior part of body yellowish tan or orange to reddish brown, variable black spots become irregular dark bands in the middle of the body; posterior part of body dark blue to black with irregular markings; short dark stripe behind each eye; males smaller and slimmer than females, with prominent pelvic spurs either side of the cloaca (cavity into which alimentary canal, genital, and urinary ducts open)

Diet: Mainly mammals such as rodents and bats, but also birds; young feed mainly on lizards; heat-sensitive pits located on each lip are used to detect warm-blooded prey

Breeding: Livebearer (gives birth to living young). The 5–40 young have pale orange bodies with dark orange to brown crossbands; adult coloration develops at about 18 months

Related endangered species: Cuban tree boa *(Epicrates angulifer)* LRnt; Puerto Rican boa *(E. inornatus)* LRnt; Virgin Islands boa *(E. monensis granti)* EN; Mona Island boa *(E. monensis monensis)* EN

Status: IUCN VU; CITES I

See also: Introductions **1:** 54; Boa, Madagascar **3:** 6; Python, Woma **8:** 6

caves or holes in limestone, and is nocturnal (active at night). Continued fragmentation of the habitat will endanger them further. One population, on Goat Island off Jamaica, has been completely destroyed by mongoose. This island once supported the endangered Jamaican iguana, which is now restricted to a small area in Hellshire on the southern coast. Part of Hellshire has been proposed for national park status. Goat Island may be restored as a habitat, but it would have to be cleared of mongoose first.

Breeding in Captivity

The problems of breeding Jamaican boas in captivity have largely been solved—a number of zoos and private keepers in the United States and Europe hold substantial numbers. The species is known to live for over 20 years in captivity and to produce sizable litters under these conditions. This should provide a good supply of young boas for reintroduction to the wild. Hope Zoo in Kingston, Jamaica, would be an ideal breeding facility, and other zoos, particularly Fort Worth Zoo in Texas, are assisting the staff in Kingston with advice.

Although IUCN listed and designated on CITES Appendix I, the boa's protection in Jamaica has left much to be desired. It was recommended for total protection over 30 years ago, but this was not fully implemented. There is a need to educate and persuade the public to protect this harmless snake. As the population and tourist industry grow, pressure on the land—and the boa's habitat—will increase.

An iridescent sheen covers the boa's body, particularly when the skin has been newly shed.

Boa, Madagascar

Acrantophis madagascariensis

Like much of Madagascar's wildlife, the Madagascar boa and its relatives are under threat from habitat destruction. Once revered and protected by the local people, the snake is now killed for its skin, which is used for making tourist souvenirs.

The subfamily Boinae contains the well-known boa constrictor of tropical America. Madagascar's three boa species are thought to have shared a common ancestor with the boa constrictor, but they grew up in isolation when Madagascar split from mainland Africa. The Madagascar boa and Dumeril's boa are usually referred to as "ground boas," whereas a third species, the Madagascar tree boa, is arboreal (although it is often seen on the ground). All three face similar problems and are listed as Vulnerable. The Madagascar boa is the larger of the two ground boas;

a possible length of 10.5 feet (3.3 m) is claimed, but 7 to 9 feet (2.1 to 2.8 m) is the average adult size. The Madagascar boa and its close relative, Dumeril's boa, are similar in appearance, but Dumeril's is rather brighter and differently patterned; it also lacks the large scales on the head that are a feature of the Madagascar boa.

Boas are carnivorous, and they kill their prey by constricting. Their appetite for rodents tends to lead them to cultivated fields and human habitation, but they are not dangerous to people.

Changing Attitudes

The Malagasy are made up of several ethnic groups, and attitudes to animals vary. Among some groups snakes have traditionally been revered since they were thought to contain the spirits of ancestors. The boas, known locally as *do*, are held in considerable awe; in certain areas the villagers are afraid to approach them, and in previous generations such beliefs prevented the killing of the animals. However, in modern times a breakdown in taboos, together with economic factors, have changed attitudes, and various animals that were once protected by taboos are now killed for food or commercial purposes. Snakeskin is used for making belts, purses, and other leather items largely for the tourist trade. Captive-bred

DATA PANEL

Madagascar boa

Acrantophis madagascariensis

Family: Boidae

World population: Unknown

Distribution: Northern Madagascar; also parts of east coast

Habitat: Moist forest regions

Size: Length: 7–9 ft (2.1–2.8 m)

Form: Snake with brownish body and variable patterns—usually a series of dark-brown lozenge shapes; sometimes spots with white centers and narrow brown bars. A distinct eye-stripe runs from the nostril through the eye on each side of the head. There is a dark blotch below each eye

Diet: Rodents and other small mammals

Breeding: Produces 2–6 live young per litter after gestation of 8–9 months. Although litters are small, young are very large

Related endangered species: Dumeril's boa (*Acrantophis dumerili*) VU; Madagascar tree boa (*Sanzinia madagascariensis*) VU

Status: IUCN VU; CITES I

COMOROS

MADAGASCAR

MOZAMBIQUE

See also: Hunting **1:** 42; Superstition **1:** 47; Boa, Jamaican **3:** 4; Python, Woma **8:** 6

The Madagascar boa *was protected for generations by local superstition. Threatened by collectors and traders, it is now preserved by conservationists.*

specimens also command high prices, but today the Madagascar boa has a CITES I listing, which means that it cannot be legally exported.

Poverty and Destruction

Much has been written about environmental destruction in Madagascar, which is mainly the result of the widespread poverty of many of its inhabitants. Land clearance for timber, agriculture, and housing has destroyed many areas, and soil erosion caused by such activities actually colors the sea red near some river mouths.

Although many areas of Madagascar are designated as wildlife reserves, the boas are in need of further protection from local people. The IUCN listing of all three Madagascar boas is based on reduction of habitat, decline in numbers, and potential exploitation of the snakes. In spite of this, there are claims that the Madagascar ground boas are reasonably plentiful, having adapted to living among secondary vegetation, including cultivated or inhabited areas. For this reason it has been suggested that a few could be exported in order to increase numbers through captive breeding.

Some are being bred privately, and several zoos in Europe and the United States hold Madagascar ground boas. All three species come under the American Zoo and Aquarium Species Survival Plan, which aims to restock a reserve in Madagascar. Dumeril's boa has been bred in substantial numbers. The tree boa produces larger litters than Dumeril's (up to 16), but does not always breed readily. The Madagascar boa is perhaps the most difficult to breed; its skin is less colorful than that of the other species, so it can be less popular with private breeders. It also has a longer gestation period and produces smaller litters. A propagation program may be set up in Madagascar, although releases would be pointless until the snakes could be better protected; the trade in snakeskin would need to be eradicated, and people educated on the harmlessness of the snakes.

7

Bowerbird, Archbold's

Archboldia papuensis

Unknown to science before 1939, Archbold's bowerbird remains one of the most elusive and enigmatic of forest birds. No one knows how many there are, but we do know that its native forests are being steadily destroyed and that its long-term survival is in question.

Archbold's bowerbird inhabits the remote and mysterious mountain forests of New Guinea. The forests are home to some of the most extraordinary birds in the world, including the spectacular birds of paradise that are famous for their fabulous plumage and breathtaking courtship displays.

Through competing with each other to attract potential mates, male birds of paradise have evolved into creatures of incomparable beauty, but at a cost. Their adornments are conspicuous and cumbersome, making them tempting targets for predators. It is perhaps no surprise that some bowerbirds, including Archbold's, have developed a courtship strategy that makes eye-catching plumage unnecessary.

Master Builders

Instead of flaunting his beauty at a potential mate, Archbold's bowerbird dazzles the female with a demonstration of his artistic skill. He builds a bower (arbor), which has the appearance of a decorated dance floor, then calls and displays until a female comes to inspect his work. If she is sufficiently impressed, she mates with him, then leaves to raise a brood while he advertizes for another female. The best builders mate with the most females, and over time competition between males has developed the building skills of some bowerbirds to an astonishing degree: The ornamented bower of one species, the Vogelkop bowerbird, is the most elaborate structure built by any animal except humans.

Although the bower of the Archbold male is not in quite the same league as that of the Vogelkop bowerbird, it is still an impressive production. The male selects an area of forest floor overhung by low branches, clears about 40 to 65 square feet (4 to 6 sq. m), and creates a mat of dry ferns, fronds, and moss. He decorates the edges of the mat with trinkets, including piles of black beetle wing cases, blue-black and gray snail shells, blue berries, and chips of amber resin from tree ferns, sometimes adding the plume of a King of Saxony bird of paradise as a final flourish. He then gathers orchid vines

DATA PANEL

Archbold's bowerbird

Archboldia papuensis

Family: Ptilonorhynchidae

World population: Unknown

Distribution: Central mountain ranges of New Guinea, mainly above 6,500 ft (2,000 m); sometimes as low as 5,600 ft (1,750 m)

Habitat: Mossy mountain forest with southern beech, Pandanus palm, tree ferns, and dense stands of bamboo

Size: Length: 14.5 in (37 cm)

Form: Large, jaylike bird with a short, stout bill. Male black with bright-yellow crest extending from forehead to neck; female dull black with ocher markings on wing primaries; juvenile male grayish with no yellow crest

Diet: Mainly fruit; also buds, flowers, seeds, succulent stems, and leaves; a few small animals

Breeding: Male is promiscuously polygamous, attracting females to mate by displaying and calling from his bower or display mat. Mated female builds a cup nest in a tree, incubating eggs and rearing young alone

Related endangered species: Fire-maned bowerbird (*Sericulus bakeri*) VU. Two other species in the bowerbird family, the tooth-billed catbird (*Ailuroedus dentirostris*) and the golden-fronted bowerbird (*Amblyornis flavifrons*), were classified by the IUCN as LRnt, but have since been removed from the list

Status: IUCN LRnt; not listed by CITES

from the forest trees and drapes them from the overhanging branches to create ground-sweeping curtains around and across the mat. His stage set, he begins his performance.

Calling with a selection of whistles, growls, and hoarse cries, he attracts a female, who usually perches on one of the overhanging branches. He then starts a strange begging, groveling display, crawling across the mat with his body and tail pressed to the ground, holding his wings partly open and churring almost continuously. Meanwhile, the female hops from perch to perch, fluttering coquettishly over his head so he has to chase her around the mat. This pursuit may be the female's way of assessing the male's fitness; if he passes the test, she mates with him, and his efforts are rewarded.

Lonely Isolation

Archbold's bowerbird lives only in the higher mountain forests of New Guinea, mainly at over 6,500 feet (2,000 m) above sea level. At such altitudes the forests are cold, misty, and damp, and the branches are festooned with epiphytic mosses (those that grow on the surface of other plants), as well as lichens, ferns, and orchids. It is a very different habitat from the lowland rain forests, and the animals that live there are so attuned to the highland conditions that they never stray down to the valleys between the mountain ridges. As a result, local populations of Archbold's bowerbird are effectively isolated on "islands" of highland habitat.

Shrinking Forest

Archbold's bowerbird is patchily distributed in the central ranges of the island, and local populations in the east are found in a small range of just 300 square miles (800 sq. km). Within this area the birds are threatened by logging in two of their forest strongholds, and as their habitats contract, the birds may soon be in trouble. Elsewhere on the island local populations seem to be larger, and their habitats are still intact, but this situation may not last.

Conservationists are concerned for the future of Archbold's bowerbird. Formerly classed as Vulnerable, it is now considered to be less at risk but is still listed as near threatened. Its IUCN classification is a clear warning that if habitat destruction from logging continues at the present rate, the bird may soon join the danger list, along with many of its unique neighbors in the mountain forests of New Guinea.

A male Archbold's bowerbird *attracts female mates by his prowess at building a decorative bower, rather than by his plumage.*

Bustard, Great

Otis tarda

Despite its vast natural range across much of Europe and Asia, the magnificent great bustard is struggling to survive as its open steppe habitats are gradually transformed by the spread of intensive farming methods.

A male great bustard displaying in the spring breeding season is an astonishing sight. The huge, stately bird suddenly upends its tail and wings to reveal great fans of snow-white feathers, while inflating its throat pouch to erect a brush of gray plumage that almost conceals its head.

This sight was once commonplace on the open steppes that originally covered vast tracts of Europe and Asia. The rolling, almost treeless plains were ideal great bustard habitat, offering the largely flightless birds freedom of movement and a wealth of food. Flocks of thousands pecked their way across the flower-rich grasslands, searching for shoots and seeds, grasshoppers, beetles, and the occasional lizard or vole.

When people started felling the forests for farmland, the bustards took the opportunity to extend their range, learning to live and breed on the newly plowed land among the crops. In the 18th century there were probably more great bustards than ever before, and in Germany children were given time off from school to help chase the hungry flocks off the fields and collect their eggs for food.

Tempting Targets

A large, meaty animal, the great bustard has always been hunted. The invention of the shotgun made it vulnerable, and by the beginning of the 19th century the birds were being slaughtered in large numbers. Today too, hunting remains a major problem; in Spain over 2,000 bustards were killed every year before they received legal protection in 1980.

Yet the main threat to the bustard's survival is more insidious than hunting. Throughout the 19th and 20th centuries agriculture became steadily more intensive as farmers found new ways of feeding crops and destroying weeds and pests. Gradually, extensive, weed-strewn fields gave way to tightly controlled blocks of farmland separated by fences and hedges. This enclosure destroyed the open, undisturbed landscapes the birds require for successful breeding. In the 1970s the screw was tightened with the widespread adoption of chemical pesticides that kill off the weeds and insects the bustards eat.

DATA PANEL

Great bustard

Otis tarda

Family: Otididae

World population: 31,000–37,000

Distribution: Scattered over the grassy plains of Morocco, Portugal, Spain, central Europe, Turkey, Russia, southwestern and Central Asia, Mongolia, and China

Habitat: Steppe grassland, pasture, and lightly wooded areas; also nonintensive farmland

Size: Length: 30–41 in (75–105 cm); wingspan: 6.2–8.5 ft (1.9–2.6 m). Weight: male up to 40 lb (18 kg); female up to 11 lb (5 kg)

Form: Large, upright, deep-chested, and robust bird with long legs and a long, thick neck. Barred black-and-gold upperparts, pale blue-gray head and neck, white underparts

Diet: Mainly young shoots, leaves, flowers, and seeds, plus insects and small vertebrates

Breeding: Male uses spectacular breeding display to attract and mate with as many females as possible. Mated females nest alone, laying 2–3 eggs in a depression on the ground in April–May. Eggs hatch in 3–4 weeks; young fledge at 4–5 weeks

Related endangered species: Great Indian bustard (*Ardeotis nigriceps*) EN; Houbara bustard (*Chlamydotis undulata*) LRnt; Bengal florican (*Houbaropsis bengalensis*) EN; lesser florican (*Sypheotides indica*) EN; little bustard (*Tetrax tetrax*) LRnt

Status: IUCN VU; CITES II

See also: Pesticides 1: 51; Money Problems 1: 88; Corncrake 3: 66; Kagu 5: 88

Plummeting Numbers

As a result, bustard numbers have crashed over the past few decades. In Hungary an estimated 8,500 in 1941 slumped to 3,400 in 1980 and shrank again to 1,100 by 1995. In Germany the 800 bustards counted in the 1970s had dwindled to 130 by 1993. In many other countries the situation is much the same. The only large, well-documented European population is in Spain, where between 17,000 and 19,000 great bustards—half the world total—still thrive on the dry grasslands. Yet even here their future is threatened by the cultivation of old pasture, building of fences, and installation of irrigation and drainage projects.

In eastern Europe and Asia the outlook is bleak. In Europe the collapse of Communism has put much of the land in private ownership, and it looks as if much of this will become farmed intensively along Western

The spectacular display of the male great bustard is a reproductive tactic designed to attract the maximum number of mates during the breeding season.

lines. There are still some 8,000 bustards in Russia, but in China and Mongolia intensive farming, grassland fires, and hunting have reduced populations to between 3,000 and 4,000.

The main hope for the great bustard lies in the reversal of the trend toward intensive, chemical-based agriculture, coupled with specific measures such as the prevention of steppe fires and illegal hunting. Providing protected areas of habitat may also help; but since the birds need to roam over large areas, they do not thrive in enclosed wildlife reserves. Ultimately, their future will probably depend on persuading farmers to conserve their unique wildlife heritage.

Butterfly, Apollo

Parnassius apollo

Apollo butterflies inhabit areas of difficult terrain and are poorly known. As a result, they have been much sought-after by collectors. There has been a dramatic drop in the number of Apollo butterflies in many areas, and the species is now protected by law in 11 European countries.

The Apollo butterfly is named after Mount Parnassus, a mountain near Delphi in Greece; one of its twin peaks was consecrated to Apollo, the most revered of the Greek gods. According to Greek mythology, Apollo is connected to light and to the sun (Apollo's first name, Phoebus, means bright).

Apollo butterflies are large and are powerful fliers. They may be seen by the fortunate observer during their June to August flight period soaring high above the hillsides, rising and falling with the air currents. Unlike birds, butterflies rarely use soaring flight, so the Apollo is unusual in this respect.

The Apollo butterfly was first described in 1741 by Charles Linnaeus, the Swedish taxonomist, when he was professor of botany at Uppsala University in Sweden. He regarded the species as uncommon in his homeland and thought that it was rarely found elsewhere. It was, in fact, widespread in mountainous areas of Europe. Farther afield, it is known in remote areas of Asia, as far as Mongolia and China.

A number of subspecies are recognized, some of which have been identified only recently. Most species of the butterfly inhabit rocky or mountainous areas above the tree line; they are rarely found in wet areas.

The Apollo is in the same family as the swallowtail butterfly, named after the distinctive "swallow tail" markings on its hind wings. The Apollo is also distinctive. Its red and black markings set against a pale background seem to be a defense against predator birds, which generally do not eat them.

The Apollo's wings are covered with a thin layer of hair, so they can appear translucent. The large size of the wings and their dark markings may help the butterflies absorb warmth from the sun's rays. The furry covering may also help retain heat.

Unusual Caterpillars

Unlike many butterflies, the caterpillar (larva) of the Apollo grows very slowly, taking nearly two years to reach pupation. During its hibernation the caterpillar spins a silk cocoon, which probably serves to protect it from winter frosts. Such behavior is unusual among butterflies.

DATA PANEL

Apollo butterfly

Parnassius apollo

Family: Papilionidae

World population: Unknown

Distribution: Europe; Scandinavia, Alps, and Pyrenees; parts of Asia

Habitat: Mountain ranges at low altitudes

Size: Length: 0.8 in (2 cm); wingspan: 2.8 in (7 cm)

Form: Butterfly with 2 pairs of wings; cream forewings with black markings; hind wings with red markings; body covered in fine scales; wings covered in hair

Diet: Adults eat nectar; caterpillars (larvae) eat alpine vegetation—stonecrops and saxifrages

Breeding: Sexes separate; males mate only once. Egg develops into caterpillar (larva), then chrysalis (pupa), then adult (butterfly)

Related endangered species: *Parnassius autocrator* (no common name) VU; swallowtail butterflies: several species, including Jordan's swallowtail (*Papilio jordani*) VU; cream-banded swallowtail (*P. leucotaenia*) VU

Status: IUCN VU; not listed by CITES

See also: Pollution **1:** 50; Butterfly, Large Blue **3:** 20; Butterfly, Large Copper **3:** 22

A related species, *Parnassius autocrator,* has a brilliant orange caterpillar that can release a most unpleasant odor from a gland behind its head. The odor acts as a defense mechanism to warn off predators. The gland, the osmaterium, is present in all Apollo and swallowtail butterfly larvae, but the odor is too faint to be detected by humans.

Sharp Decline

The Apollo has declined rapidly and is considered rare or endangered throughout Europe. It is now protected by law in 11 European countries.

Among the natural factors that may also be contributing to the decline of Apollo populations are threats from parasites on caterpillars, predators, and competitors for its food. However, many theories for the decline of the Apollo butterfly relate to environmental damage resulting from human activity. They include acid rain caused by pollution, modern agricultural practices, pollution of food plants by traces of heavy metals, overcollecting by enthusiasts, and climate change.

While the exact reasons for the Apollo's decline are still unclear, scientists have discovered that it is quite easy to breed the butterflies. The caterpillars feed on orpine, a species of stonecrop—succulent perennial plants with purplish-white flowers.

Scientific research has assisted in Apollo conservation, and established restoration programs are now underway in several European countries. They include three activities: restoration of former habitats, preparation of suitable new ones, and captive-breeding programs. Researchers are studying the basic conditions needed for successful breeding and population maintenance, especially the climatic requirements of the Apollo butterflies, their preferred grassland habitats, and the abundance and distribution of orpine.

The Apollos, *like the festoons and swallowtails of the same family, are characterized by their bright markings and have the capacity for powerful flight. They are endangered throughout Europe, but breeding programs are enabling numbers to recover.*

Butterfly, Avalon Hairstreak

Strymon avalona

The Avalon hairstreak butterfly is named after the town of Avalon on Santa Catalina Island off the coast of southern California. The butterfly is rare, and careful conservation measures are now needed to preserve its habitat and host plants.

Hairstreak butterflies are so called because most species have a fine, light-colored row of dots or hairlike markings running across the underside of both the fore and hind wing, which is visible when the insect is settled with its wings up. The butterflies also have one or more small, taillike extensions on their hind wings.

Hairstreak butterflies are found in Europe, North America, and temperate Asia; the ranges of some North American species extend into South America. Generally, the butterflies do not stray into areas inhabited by people, so they are better seen in woods and open countryside rather than in suburban areas and gardens. Hairstreaks include species with very local distributions. The butterflies' flight is fast and erratic, and they always settle with the wings closed, thus hiding the coloration of the upper surface. The tails on the hind wings may have an interesting function in confusing predators. Although those on the Avalon hairstreak are relatively short, in some of its Asiatic relatives they are long and twisted. When the insects settle, the tails are often made to quiver or tremble, and it is thought that some predators mistake them for antennae, thus believing the butterfly is positioned back to front. Attacks on the false antennae tails are less likely to be fatal to the animal than those to the real antennae situated on the head.

The species of hairstreak butterflies that live in temperate regions usually produce one batch of young each year. A few survive the winter as chrysalises or pupae, but the majority do so as eggs, ready to hatch when the weather and plant growth improve. The tropical species reproduce throughout the year, taking only a few weeks to complete their lifecycles.

The caterpillars of many hairstreaks are attended by ants, who "milk" them for honeydew. The ants stroke the caterpillars with their antennae and forelegs. The stimulation encourages the caterpillars to

DATA PANEL

Avalon hairstreak butterfly

Strymon avalona

Family: Lycaenidae

World population: Unknown

Distribution: Catalina Island, California

Habitat: Chaparral (dense area of shrubs, brushwood, and trees, especially evergreen oaks, in southwestern U.S.); grassy areas

Size: Wingspan: 0.7–1 in (1.9–2.5 cm)

Form: Typical butterfly. Two pairs of wings; each hind wing bears 1 short "tail." Upper side of wings grayish; upper side of hind wings bear yellow or red spot near the tail and may have small, whitish spots near the edge. Fine, light row of dots or hairline markings on underside of both wings

Diet: Caterpillars feed on silverleaf lotus and deerbrush lotus. Adults feed on nectar from common summac and giant buckwheat

Breeding: Female lays round, flat eggs on terminal and flower bud of silverleaf lotus, island broom, or deerbrush lotus. Sluglike caterpillars (larvae) emerge from February to December

Related endangered species: No close relatives, but 3 other hairstreaks in the U.S. may face similar threats

Status: IUCN VU; not listed by CITES

14

See also: Communities and Ecosystems **1:** 22; What Is a Species? **1:** 26; Butterfly, Hermes Copper **3:** 18

release a sticky, sugary secretion, which the ants eat. In return the ants give the caterpillars protection from small insect predators.

Hairstreak butterflies usually lay eggs that are round and flattened, appearing like minute cookies. With the help of a good lens it is possible to make out geometrical patterns on the eggs. The patterns vary between species. When the caterpillars emerge, they look rather sluglike in shape. They feed on the flowers and leaves of trees and bushes rather than on herbaceous plants.

In the case of the Avalon hairstreak butterfly, which is one of the rarest and most isolated butterfly species in the United States, the female lays her eggs at the end of the stems and on the flower buds of the silverleaf lotus plant. The lotus has silvery-green leaves and clusters of orange flowers. The female also lays eggs on the island broom or deerbrush lotus, with its rich, green foliage and clusters of yellow and orange flowers. Hatching takes place between February and December, when broods of caterpillars emerge from the eggs to feed on the plants. Toward the end of the hatching period adults may also be seen. The adults feed on nectar from the bunches of small, cream-white flowers of the laurel or common sumac. They also take nectar from the flowers of the giant buckwheat or St. Catharine's lace. St. Catharine's lace is only found on Santa Catalina.

Isolated Existence

The Avalon hairstreak is endemic to Santa Catalina Island, which means it is found nowhere else. The isolated position of the island has allowed the butterfly to survive free from pressures such as predators or competition by species with similar requirements. Such pressures may have led to the butterfly's extinction on

The Avalon hairstreak *has a row of fine, pale hairline markings on the underside of its wings and thin, taillike extensions on the hind wings.*

the mainland. It is possible, however, that the Avalon hairstreak may have evolved on Santa Catalina Island.

The need for conservation of the Avalon hairstreak is appreciated by the authorities, who have done much to publicize its vulnerability.

15

Butterfly, Birdwing

Ornithoptera alexandrae; O. richmondia

For many years the large, tropical birdwing butterflies have been eagerly sought by collectors, and some birdwings now change hands for substantial sums of money, either legally or illegally. Many are now threatened, and their conservation is hindered by a lack of knowledge of their habits.

Some birdwing butterflies are very large; the Queen Alexandra's birdwing from Papua New Guinea is, in fact, the largest butterfly in the world, with a wingspan of almost 11 inches (27.5 cm). The Richmond birdwing from Australia, on the other hand, is one of the smaller birdwings, with a wingspan of less than 6 inches (15 cm).

The butterflies' common name is a result of their size and shape; at one time they were said to be shot by hunters who mistook them for birds. As in other *Ornithoptera* species, the sexes differ in color as well as in size: Queen Alexandra males are powder blue, green, gold, and black, and Richmond males are

shades of iridescent green and black. The females of both species are dark brown, spotted with white and cream. Female birdwings are generally larger than their male counterparts, although their coloration is less spectacular.

The butterflies have adapted to forest habitats where occasional flowers provide enough nectar to feed the adults. The males exploit certain tall trees as vantage points and as mating sites. Females move around between patches of rain forest in search of specific vines on which to lay their eggs.

Birdwing butterflies have long been favorites with collectors. When all the species were listed by CITES, making it illegal for them to be offered for sale, a lucrative trade in smuggled specimens developed, with single Queen Alexandra's birdwings fetching more than $500 on the black market. Protection from collecting has done little by itself, however, to improve the butterflies' prospects, since the numbers actually changing hands are now small.

Habitat Destruction

A much greater threat comes from the destruction of their habitats and the food plants they live on. Birdwing caterpillars feed selectively on certain species of tropical forest vine belonging to the genus *Aristolochia*. These vines occur only in rain forest and frequently have a rather patchy distribution, especially where they have suffered from human interference in the form of timber-felling or forest clearing for urban development or farming. Over the past

---

DATA PANEL

Birdwing butterfly: Queen Alexandra's birdwing; Richmond birdwing

Ornithoptera alexandrae; O. richmondia

Family: Papilionidae

World population: Unknown

Distribution: Queen Alexandra's birdwing: Papua New Guinea. Richmond birdwing: subtropical Queensland and New South Wales, Australia

Habitat: Open woodland and tropical rain forest

Size: Wingspan: Queen Alexandra's birdwing: up to 11 in (27.5 cm). Richmond birdwing: less than 6 in (15 cm)

Form: Large butterflies with 2 pairs of conspicuous wings, the leading pair much longer than the second

Diet: Caterpillars feed on forest vine of genus *Aristolochia*; adults on nectar

Breeding: Eggs laid singly on upper side of leaves of host plant; they hatch into caterpillars that feed on plant for about 4 weeks before developing into a chrysalis. Chrysalis hatches into adult butterfly after about 3 weeks

Related endangered species: Obi birdwing butterfly (*Ornithoptera aesacus*) VU; Rothschild's birdwing butterfly (*O. Rothschildi*) VU

Status: Queen Alexandra's birdwing IUCN EN; CITES I. Richmond's birdwing not listed by IUCN. Birdwing butterflies (*Ornithoptera* spp.) CITES II

See also: Communities and Ecosystems 1: 22; What Is a Species? 1: 26; butterfly species 3: 12–23

10 years some important species of the vines have become scarce except in a few national parks, which are not always large enough to guarantee their long-term survival.

The loss of the vines has in turn threatened some of the birdwing species with extinction. The Queen Alexandra's and Richmond birdwings face particularly severe problems. Both have relatively small distributions that are especially vulnerable to forest clearance and the disappearance of food plants and breeding grounds.

Queen Alexandra's birdwing larvae apparently feed exclusively on a particular species of the vine *Aristolochia dielsiana*. Although the vine is widely distributed in Papua New Guinea, it is only available in sufficient quantities to support the huge, ravenous Queen Alexandra's caterpillars in the province of Oro.

Only Oro has enough of the volcanic, phosphate-rich soils that the vines need if they are to flourish. Richmond birdwing larvae depend on another vine, *A. praevenosa*. Their only natural food plant is found in lowland rain forests. However, at higher altitudes—above 2,500 feet (800 m)—on the border ranges of Queensland and New South Wales the Richmond birdwing larvae may also feed on a variant subspecies of *A. deltantha*.

Only when research has figured out all such complexities will biologists fully understand the life cycle of the remarkable birdwing butterflies. Yet such knowledge is necessary if strategies are to be designed to protect them.

Brilliant colors *mark the Richmond birdwing (above) and the Queen Alexandra's birdwing (right), shown here emerging from its chrysalis.*

Butterfly, Hermes Copper

Lycaena hermes

The Hermes copper is an endangered butterfly with a distribution limited to the district around San Diego and the adjacent northern end of Baja California. It is especially susceptible to habitat damage by developers and fire.

California is home to a great number of butterfly species. Over 100 have been recorded from Orange County alone. The wide range of habitats found in the state, from barren open or wooded mountains through cool river gorges to hot coastal plains and offshore islands, means that there have been many opportunities for new species to evolve in specialized habitats. In some cases the habitats are fragile and are now subject to pressures from development; in others the areas are small (like some offshore islands) and so are also vulnerable.

The California Department of Fish and Game is concerned for the future of 55 species of butterfly that are listed as rare or endangered within the state. Their concerns are shared by the United States Fish and Wildlife Service, especially where the future of breeding rests on many small, separate populations.

One such species is the Hermes copper, a member of the family Lycaenidae (gossamer-winged butterflies). The family is represented by about 100 species in North America and has four groups: the coppers, the blues, the hairstreaks, and the harvesters. A relative of the highly restricted and endangered Avalon hairstreak butterfly, the Hermes copper occurs around San Diego and at the northern end of Baja California. Although not striking in appearance, the Hermes copper has one spikelike tail on each of its hind wings, giving it a slightly swallowtail appearance. It can be confused with hairstreak butterflies, so its wing markings are important in identification.

Like many Californian butterflies, the Hermes copper relies on a specialized habitat with particular plants and climate, so its geographical distribution is local and patchy. It inhabits woodlands, preferably where there is a good mix of tree species, chaparral (dense growth of shrubs and trees), and coastal sage scrub. Such habitats provide the necessary plant hosts, including the redberry of the buckthorn family, for caterpillars to feed on. The butterflies have survived close to suburban San Diego as a result of the buckthorn's distribution. The adults feed on nectar from the flowers of wild buckwheat.

DATA PANEL

Hermes copper butterfly

Lycaena hermes

Family: Lycaenidae

World population: Unknown

Distribution: California; range restricted to San Diego County and adjacent Baja California

Habitat: Mixed woodlands, chaparral (dense growth of shrubs and trees), and coastal scrub

Size: Wingspan: 1–1.3 in (2.5–3.2 cm)

Form: Typical butterfly; 2 pairs of conspicuous wings; each hind wing bears 1 short "tail." Upper side brown with yellow-orange patch surrounding black spots; underside bright yellow; forewing with 4–6 black spots; hind wing with 3–6 black spots. Caterpillars (larvae) are apple to dark green and have much simpler eyes than adult butterflies

Diet: Caterpillars feed on redberry. Adults feed on nectar from flowers of wild buckwheat

Breeding: Male settles on plants to watch for females. Single eggs are laid on twigs of caterpillar host plant, redberry; pupae hatch from end of May to mid-June. After hatching, the young caterpillars feed on the new young shoots of host plant

Related endangered species: Avalon hairstreak butterfly (*Strymon avalona*)* VU

Status: IUCN VU; not listed by CITES

UNITED STATES

MEXICO

See also: Populations 1: 20; Pesticides 1: 51; Butterfly, Avalon Hairstreak 3: 14; Butterfly, Large Copper 3: 22

Hermes copper butterflies have good eyesight, which is important in the mating behavior. They have a pair of typical insect compound "eyes" on the head consisting of many individual visual units (known as omatidia). Moving and static objects can be viewed accurately. The markings on the butterfly's wings are important in the recognition of members of the same species and the initiation of mating behavior. Male butterflies perch on twigs looking out for females to mate with. Eggs are laid singly on the twigs of the host plant and do not hatch until the following spring. At this time of year the young leaf buds on the host plant are shooting and able to provide the necessary food for the caterpillars.

Habitat Hazards

Increasing urban growth is causing a serious problem for wildlife in California and other rapidly developing parts of the United States. The construction of domestic and industrial building sites, new roads, and electricity lines causes fragmentation—the breaking up of habitats into smaller and smaller sectors. The fragmented areas become separated by man-made barriers, and wild animals are not able to move around as freely as they once could. As a result, individual breeding groups become isolated from each other. Some wild species, including insects such as butterflies, become restricted to remnants of habitat that are no longer big enough to support them. This reduces the overall breeding strength of the population.

Another major problem for butterfly colonies is forest fires. Fires start easily in the dry climate, and the butterflies, along with their food plants, are constantly at risk. The continued widespread use of pesticides

Hermes copper butterflies *in flight and at rest, displaying the species' distinctive wing markings.*

and herbicides is also damaging to adult butterflies, their caterpillars, and their food plants.

The Hermes copper is listed locally as rare or local throughout its range, and a strategy is needed to protect it from further habitat loss and fragmentation. An increase in public awareness, particularly among local government officers and within the construction industry, would greatly help its future.

Butterfly, Large Blue

Maculinea arion

The large blue butterfly is so called because of the distinctive turquoise-blue sheen on parts of its wings. Its life cycle is inextricably linked with other insect species and plant life, making it vulnerable to natural or human disturbance of any kind.

The large blue butterfly is found scattered over Europe, particularly in coastal areas. It is capable of vigorous flight, despite its fragile appearance, and can navigate strong winds that would make flying difficult for other insects.

Like other butterflies, the large blue begins life as an egg. The female lays her clutch on the leaves of wild thyme, having carefully selected the site. As well as having the right microclimate, or balance of humidity, protection, and temperature, the bush must be close to or on top of an ant's nest, because of the large blue's dependency on ant larvae for food.

The eggs hatch into caterpillars—the second stage of the butterfly's life cycle. When they first emerge, the caterpillars are well camouflaged, closely resembling the white thyme blossom on which they feed. They molt, or shed their skin, up to four times, growing rapidly after the earlier molts. After the second they become carnivorous, leaving the thyme plant to hunt for insects. They may also feed on caterpillars of the same species.

At the caterpillar stage the large blue butterfly frequently encounters ants. A relationship with the ant community develops, and the caterpillar begins to rely for its development on ant larvae. The ants, in turn, benefit from the caterpillar's dependency, relishing the honeydew secreted by a gland on its abdomen. The ant strokes the gland to stimulate secretion and drinks the honeydew produced. The caterpillar then hunches up, signaling that it is ready to be carried to the ants' nest. The ants take the caterpillar deep down into the nest, where it is tended to by worker ants and milked for honeydew. Secure in the nest, the caterpillar starts to feed on ant larvae. Incredibly, the worker ants who usually guard the larvae fiercely allow the predation to carry on. Cases of ant colonies dying out because they could not support a large volume of large blue caterpillars have been recorded.

After about six weeks the caterpillar has changed into a white, fleshy, grublike animal. In this state it hibernates throughout the winter, developing into a chrysalis (pupa) in May. After three weeks' pupation, during which it undergoes dramatic

---

DATA PANEL

Large blue butterfly

Maculinea arion

Family: Lycaenidae

World population: Unknown

Distribution: Europe

Habitat: Coastal areas and downland; also mountains up to 6,560 ft (2,000 m)

Size: Length: 0.7 in (1.7 cm); wingspan: 1.6 in (4 cm)

Form: Body covered in fine scales. Two pairs of conspicuous wings with black patterns on blue background; underside of wings brown with black marks (females have more marks on front wings than males); each mark is surrounded by a fine white ring

Diet: At the caterpillar stage the large blue butterfly eats wild thyme blossom, insects (including other caterpillars), and ant larvae. Adults feed on flower nectar and other liquids

Breeding: Female lays eggs in wild thyme flowers. Egg develops into caterpillar (larva), then chrysalis (pupa), and finally adult butterfly. Adults emerge as separate sexes

Related endangered species: Large copper butterfly (*Lycaena dispar*)* LRnt; Avalon hairstreak butterfly (*Strymon avalona*)* VU

Status: IUCN LRnt; not listed by CITES

See also: Specialization 1: 28; Butterfly, Apollo 3: 12; Butterfly, Large Copper 3: 22

internal changes, it
emerges from its cocoon as
an adult large blue and leaves the
ants' nest, making its way through the
maze of passages until it reaches the outside
world. The larvae of most other blue butterfly species
have the honey glands and attract ants, but unlike the
large blue, are not taken into the ants' nests.

Dangers

The large blue butterfly's dependence on particular
plant and insect life makes survival problematic. Its
preference for just one type of plant for egg laying
means that it is totally reliant on an abundance of wild
thyme. Scarcity of the plant because of human
encroachment could severely threaten the species.
Wild thyme also appears to offer the right
microclimate for speedy development of the eggs,
thereby reducing exposure to predators. Another

The large blue butterfly *feeds on nectar from flowers,*
using its long proboscis or tongue to draw up the liquid.

concern is the tendency of the caterpillars to feed on
their own kind when they become carnivorous. Such
behavior can have an adverse effect on numbers
reaching adulthood.

Codependency with ants is essential to the life
cycle of the large blue. In parts of Europe human
disturbance of heathland, by building, for example,
has wiped out ant nests. Such activity has limited the
number of suitable sites for the large blue butterfly.

Butterfly, Large Copper

Lycaena dispar

The large copper butterfly was introduced into Britain from the Netherlands in 1927 to replace the native established English race that had become extinct in about 1850. In Britain the species is found in only one locality, where it is protected; in the Netherlands it may well be extinct.

The large copper butterfly is an example of a species that is highly adapted to a particular habitat. It relies on the availability of fens and marshes, favoring only one species of marsh vegetation: the great water dock plant. The butterfly uses the plant as a site for egg laying and as a source of food. The caterpillars may also feed on sorrel.

Once the eggs have been laid, the developing larvae (caterpillars) feed on the underside of the leaves, remaining hidden from view. As they feed they gradually cut holes in the leaves. As winter approaches, they hibernate, changing from the soft green color of the feeding phase to the brownish-purple of the hibernating phase. The lack of fresh chlorophyll (green pigment) in the leaves is probably the cause of this. To some extent their drab color matches that of the decaying leaves of the great water dock as the plant dies down in winter.

Astonishingly, the larvae can withstand immersion in water during the winter floods. With the onset of spring the larvae resume feeding and also regain their soft green color. Immediately before they pupate, the caterpillars spin a pad of silk thread on a leaf and attach themselves to it.

Large copper butterfly larvae do not secrete honeydew and lack the honey gland found in some species. Instead, they produce a sweet secretion from the skin. This attracts ants that protect the larvae from various parasites and predators.

Shrinking Habitat

The large copper butterfly was once fairly widespread in the fens of East Anglia, Lincolnshire, and Cambridgeshire in eastern England. However, habitat destruction

DATA PANEL

Large copper butterfly

Lycaena dispar

Family: Lycaenidae

World population: Unknown

Distribution: Europe

Habitat: Fen (low-lying, flat marshy land) and marsh

Size: Length head/body: 0.8 in (1.7 cm); wingspan: 1.8 in (4.3 cm)

Form: Two pairs of conspicuous wings. Males and females have (different) copper and black-colored markings on the upper wings; underside of wings similar in both sexes. Wings and body are covered with fine scales

Diet: Adults feed on liquids such as nectar, using sucking mouthparts. Larvae (caterpillars) feed on leaves of the great water dock

Breeding: Eggs laid in summer develop into larvae, which live through the winter. Pupae develop and metamorphose into males or females in late June

Related endangered species: Hermes copper *(Lycaena hermes)** VU

Status: IUCN LRnt; not listed by CITES

See also: Reintroduction **1:** 92; Butterfly, Apollo **3:** 12; Butterfly, Hermes Copper **3:** 18

and overcollection by zealous butterfly enthusiasts (supported by local people selling them) exerted pressure on the large copper and contributed to its extinction. The Continental strain of large copper butterfly, which was introduced to Britain from the Netherlands, is now becoming established; if attempts had been made to conserve the habitat of the native strain when it was dying out in the late 1840s, the original English race might still exist.

The large copper butterfly's reliance on a particular habitat makes the species extremely vulnerable to environmental change. Drainage of wetlands and woodland development

destroy the vegetation required by the larvae. In addition, suitable sites are often widely separated from each other by inhospitable habitat, so expansion of populations is difficult.

Conservation Plan

As long as the full life cycle of the large copper butterfly is understood and the needs of the egg-laying adults and larvae are catered to, conservation of the species is perfectly possible. Although the importance of habitat preservation was not appreciated in the mid-19th century, the butterfly is now the subject of a government-backed conservation plan. It is hoped that protection of this kind will allow the species to flourish.

The large copper butterfly has brilliantly colored black and copper markings and is capable of strong, rapid flight.

Camel, Wild Bactrian

Camelus bactrianus

At one time, two-humped Bactrian camels roamed widely across the open plains and deserts of central Asia. Now only a few truly wild Bactrian camels remain, although domestic examples are abundant.

The two-humped Bactrian camel lives alone or in small herds of females and their young led by an older male. The species can exist on the most unpromising diet of dry thorn bushes, salty vegetation, even bones and old shoes if necessary! They are able to withstand extremely cold winters, with temperatures below -13°F (-25°C), and searing summer heat over 95°F (35°C). Their soft, tough feet allow them to jog comfortably over rocks, snow, or loose sand, and they can accelerate to over 20 miles per hour (35 km/h) for short bursts. They can also go without water for days—or even weeks—then drink 20 gallons (90 l) or more in one go. In winter, when the water is frozen, they may exist on the plentiful moisture contained in their food. After it rains, the camels eat well, storing up to 80 lb (35 kg) of fat in each of their two humps. This acts as a food reserve in lean periods, during which time the fat is used up, and the humps become floppy and droop to one side.

Valuable Commodities

Bactrian camels can travel over 30 miles (50 km) in a day, carrying a quarter of a ton of goods. They were first domesticated about 4,500 years ago and for centuries were the main form of transport used on the Silk Route, bringing trade goods from China to the West. From about one year old, camels are capable of responding to spoken commands given by humans. They can be tamed and used to help transport people and their belongings over long distances in the harsh terrain. Consequently, there are now more than 2 million domesticated Bactrian camels, so the species is unlikely to die out—it is far too valuable.

Camels are also valuable for their meat and milk, produced from their diet of rough desert vegetation. Fat from the hump can be used for cooking; their dried dung can be burned as fuel; the fur can be made into heavy cloth, and the skins turned into useful leather.

Most domestic camels are left to wander about and fend for themselves for much of the time. Truly wild camels were widespread in the Gobi Desert until early in the 20th century. However, many were shot by poachers and all were forced to compete with increasing numbers of sheep, goats, and horses for the sparse vegetation. Domestic camels needed to be fed too, leaving little for their wild relatives. For a time it was believed that the wild camels had died out, but they were rediscovered in 1957. Surveys carried out between 1995 and 1996 suggest that there are

See also: National Parks **1:** 92; Vicuña **10:** 28; Yak, Wild **10:** 90; Zebra, Grevy's **10:** 92

The wild Bactrian camel *is named after Bactria, an ancient country in southwestern Asia. The species is now close to extinction in the wild.*

between 350 and 500 wild camels in northwestern China. The numbers had declined by 75 percent in the 15 years since a previous survey. Despite legal protection, the camels are highly endangered due to hunting and habitat destruction resulting from mining activities. Surveys in southwestern Mongolia in 1997 suggest that there may be only a few hundred camels remaining there, making a total of fewer than 1,000 Bactrian camels living in a truly wild state. The Mongolian population is spread over more than 10,000 square miles (26,000 sq. km) and has been protected from shooting since 1926: Now much of its range is within the boundaries of a national park.

DATA PANEL

Wild Bactrian camel

Camelus bactrianus

Family: Camelidae

World population: Fewer than 1,000

Distribution: Northwestern China and Mongolia (formerly widespread in arid areas of Central Asia and Mongolia)

Habitat: Desert and rocky valleys

Size: Length head body: about 10 ft (3.5 m); tail: 12–18 in (35–55 cm); height at shoulder: 6–7 ft (1.8–2.3 m). Weight: 700–1,500 lb (300–700 kg)

Form: Camel with long neck and large, bulging eyes with long eyelashes. The 2 humps on the back contain fat and often droop to one side.

Gray-brown hair grows to 10 in (25 cm) on the head, neck, forelimbs, and hump. The feet have two broad toes that are widely splayed to prevent the camel from sinking into soft ground

Diet: Vegetarian, but normally not very fussy and will eat almost anything

Breeding: Mating season toward the end of the year; most births in March–April; gestation period of 12–14 months; 1 young born every other year. Life span 30–50 years

Related endangered species: Vicuña (*Vicugna vicugna*)* LRcd; guanaco (*Lama guanicöe*) VU

Status: IUCN EN; CITES I

Caracolera, Mojarra

Nandopsis bartoni

Many Central and South American cichlids (family Cichlidae) are loved by fish enthusiasts the world over because of their beautiful colors, fascinating breeding behavior, and intense parental care of eggs and offspring. The mojarra caracolera is not only colorful, but as a parent it ranks among the very best. Sadly, wild populations are under threat from other cichlids.

The Rio Verde Valley is situated some 3,300 feet (1,000 m) above sea level in the Mexican state of San Luis de Potosí. In prehistoric times it was the site of a large lake, which, over time, disappeared, leaving behind a wide plain pockmarked with springs. Eventually, some of the springs gave rise to lagoons such as the Laguna Media Luna (Half Moon Lagoon), which is home to several cichlid species, among them the mojarra caracolera.

Confusing Names

Confusingly, there are two distinct cichlid species that are referred to as mojarra caracolera. According to the IUCN, the name applies to Barton's cichlid (*Cichlasoma bartoni*). The generic name *Cichlasoma,* however, has been the focus of great attention over the years and has resulted in a number of former *Cichlasoma* species being transferred to other genera. In the case of the mojarra caracolera a 1996 revision moved it to the genus *Herichthys*; other interpretations place it in the genus *Nandopsis*. So while the species name *bartoni* remains unchanged, three versions of the scientific name exist.

There is also some difference of opinion regarding the common name. The IUCN lists the species as mojarra caracolera (a Spanish/Mexican name), while other sources call it mojarra de dos colores (the two-colored mojarra). These other authorities use the name mojarra caracolera for a closely related species, variously known as *Cichlasoma, Herichthys,* or *Nandopsis labridens*, whose English common name is the toothlip cichlid. The IUCN, however, lists the common name simply as mojarra.

Adding further to the confusion, both species were once regarded as one and the same, and both occur in Laguna Media Luna. In addition, they are both considered to be under considerable threat in the wild.

DATA PANEL

Mojarra caracolera (Barton's cichlid)

Nandopsis bartoni

Family: Cichlidae

World population: About 10,000

Distribution: Water bodies, including Laguna Media Luna in Rio Verde Valley, San Luis de Potosí, Mexico

Habitat: Springs, streams, and lagoons mostly with clear water; vegetation, including water lilies; the substratum (bottom) is often coverd with detritus

Size: Length: about 7 in (18 cm)

Form: Body compressed; males develop hump on the head as they mature. In both sexes the lower half of the body becomes black at breeding time; the top half is white or gray-blue. At other times their bodies have a pattern of irregular vertical dark bands

Diet: Encrusting algae; will also take aquatic invertebrates

Breeding: Lays eggs in caves or close to a rock. Several hundred adhesive eggs are laid and guarded by the female; the male will defend the territory. Hatching occurs after 2 days; both parents protect the fry (baby fish) during the first few days, until they become free-swimming and disperse

Related endangered species: Mojarra caracolera de Cuatro Ciénegas (*Herichthys* or *Cichlasoma minckleyi*) VU; mojarra (*Cichlasoma,* probably *Herichthys pantostictum*) VU; also known as mojarra, (*Nandopsis labridens*) EN; Steindachner's cichlid (*N. steindachneri*) VU; mojarra de Bulha (*N. urophthalmus ericymba*) DD

Status: IUCN VU; not listed by CITES

Mojarra caracolera *are attractive fish that are highly sought after by aquarium-keeping hobbyists.*

Exotic Threats

It appears that habitat degradation in the form of pollution or water extraction does not pose any real danger to either of the mojarras. However, the introduction of a number of exotic (nonnative) species to the region undoubtedly does. The degree of threat ranges from none at all, as in the small introduced livebearing species the Tamesí molly, to very significant—as in the case of the gold dust tilapia, which was introduced as a food species for people.

A further exotic, the pearl cichlid, is known to hybridize with one of the mojarras (*N. labridens*), so posing an additional threat. It is not known if hybridization with *N. bartoni* has occurred in the wild, or even if it is possible. However, the risk cannot be discounted since the biological relationship between the two mojarras is extremely close. Interestingly, there appear to be no records of hybridization between the two mojarra species themselves.

There are several threats from the introduced cichlids. As well as competing for space, the nonnative species also compete with the mojarras for food. In addition, predation on mojarra eggs and young also seems to be taking its toll, particularly at times when food is in short supply. Predation by another introduced species, the largemouth bass—a sport and food fish—exerts yet more pressure, while shoals of the small, native Mexican tetra may prey on very young mojarras.

The cumulative effect of all the threats can be seen in declining numbers of both mojarra species, although it is more pronounced in *N. labridens*. Over the past decade or so the decline has been estimated at about 20 percent for *N. bartoni* and as high as 50 percent in *N. labridens*, with further similar drops envisaged over the next 10 years. As the populations decrease, the distribution of remaining stocks will become more fragmented, and this in turn will affect their reproductive capacity overall.

Today fewer than 10,000 individuals of *N. bartoni* remain throughout the range; no figures are available for *N. labridens*. Fortunately, both species are bred in considerable numbers commercially throughout the world, primarily to cater to aquarium keepers.

Cassowary, Southern

Casuarius casuarius

The huge, flightless southern cassowary is among the largest of all bird species. With continuing concerted conservation efforts—including habitat protection, the control of predators, and the reduction of disease—the southern cassowary's future may be safeguarded.

The southern cassowary is the largest land animal in New Guinea. It is one of three similar species of large, flightless birds on the island, but the only one that is also found in Australia. Populations of southern cassowary in Australia have declined by more than 20 percent over 30 years. An estimated total of 2,000 birds in 14 subpopulations remain in the rain forests of coastal northeastern Queensland, in part of the remote, sparsely populated Cape York Peninsula, and farther south in an area between Cooktown and Townsville. In New Guinea the species is more widespread and occurs throughout most of the lowlands. Nonetheless, it may have experienced large declines here as well.

Distinctive Features

Along with its highly modified feathers that are like luxuriant mammal hair, a distinctive feature of the southern cassowary is the blade-shaped protuberance (casque) on the top of the head. There are several theories about the casque's function. It is most likely that, along with the bare skin and wattles (loose folds of skin hanging from the neck), it plays a vital role in social behavior. Perhaps the most unlikely theory is that the bird uses it to hack through jungle vegetation. Captive individuals have been seen to use the casque as a shovel; in the wild the birds may use it to move leaf litter when searching for food.

Cassowaries have long had great cultural importance for the forest tribes of New Guinea, featuring in their legends and mystical rituals. As well as hunting them for their meat, the people use their feathers for ceremonial headdresses, make the quills of their primary wing feathers into earrings or nosepins, and carve the leg bones into daggers, spoons, or other implements. Villagers often keep the birds in captivity, taking them as chicks and feeding them until they are large enough to provide a substantial meal or to sell to a trader. As soon as they reach adulthood, if not before, the birds are securely penned.

DATA PANEL

Southern cassowary (double-wattled, two-wattled, common, or Australian cassowary)

Casuarius casuarius

Family: Casuariidae

World population: Fewer than 10,000 individuals

Distribution: New Guinea, both in Papua (formerly Irian Jaya), Indonesia, and Papua New Guinea, as well as Indonesian islands of Aru and Seram; parts of northeastern Australia

Habitat: Rain forests, fruit plantations, savanna, and mangroves near forest

Size: Height: up to 5.5 ft (1.7 m). Weight: male 64–75 lb (29–34 kg); female 128 lb (58 kg)

Form: Heavy-bodied, flightless bird covered with glossy, black, hairlike plumage. Primary wingtip feathers—modified as strong, bare quills—curve under body, head, and neck. Pale-blue bare skin on head, darker blue on neck with variable red areas; 2 fleshy red wattles hang from foreneck. Casque protrudes from top of head; female has brighter bare areas and bigger casque; bare parts vary in color with mood. Chicks have yellow and black stripes; immatures brown with smaller casque and wattles

Diet: Mainly fruit; also fungi, snails, insects and other invertebrates; sometimes small vertebrates or carrion

Breeding: After mating, female spends a few weeks with male in his territory; 3–5 dark-green eggs laid in shallow nest built by male. Female mates with other males, leaving each in turn to incubate eggs alone for about 7 weeks; male cares for chicks for about 9 months

Related endangered species: Dwarf cassowary *(Casuarius bennetti)* LRnt; northern cassowary *(C. unappendiculatus)* VU

Status: IUCN VU; not listed by CITES

New Guinea

INDONESIA

PAPUA NEW GUINEA

AUSTRALIA

See also: Research **1:** 84; Kiwi, Brown **6:** 8

Although they prefer to escape from danger by running away—their powerful legs and feet enable them to move at up to 30 miles per hour (50 km/h)—cassowaries can be dangerous when defending young or when cornered, as sometimes happens with captive birds. The innermost toe on each foot bears a razor-sharp, daggerlike claw measuring 4 inches (10 cm). The cassowary uses the claw as a formidable weapon.

Threats

Hunting poses a significant threat to the southern cassowary in New Guinea, although populations can remain viable where the birds are regularly trapped. As well as destroying habitat, logging has opened up new areas to hunters. In Australia the main threat was, until recently, the rapid destruction of areas of rain forest. The remaining subpopulations are isolated by the fragmentation of their habitat and are vulnerable to being hit by vehicles as they cross roads. The birds are also at risk from disease, hunting (to protect crops or for food and sport), and predation by dogs (and perhaps pigs). The pigs may also compete with the birds for food or degrade their habitat.

Conservation

Conservationists have set targets for the protection of the southern cassowary in both Irian Jaya and Papua New Guinea. They include monitoring populations, analyzing the effects of hunting and logging on numbers, and encouraging hunting restrictions.

In Australia similar initiatives exist, and most cassowary habitat is now protected by law. There is still a need to improve monitoring techniques and to research population dynamics. The priorities are the control of predators, the prevention of habitat destruction and disease, and the reduction of road deaths. Fortunately, the destruction of rain forests in Australia has declined, while in New Guinea there are still large areas that are as yet unaffected by hunting or habitat destruction.

The cassowary's *razor-sharp claw (inset) is a fine weapon. When launching an attack, it rears up at or runs past its victim, kicking out with both feet and slashing anybody in its path. Its claws can inflict a serious or even fatal injury.*

Cat, Iriomote

Mayailurus iriomotensis

First described in 1967, the rare Iriomote cat has been at the center of a classification debate ever since. The controversy has implications for scientists, conservationists, and politicians, not to mention the cats themselves.

The small island of Iriomote is one of the least developed places in Japan. People only began to live there after World War II, when newly developed insecticides such as DDT made it possible to control the mosquitoes. The people who settled on Iriomote soon became familiar with the island's native cat, and it was a frequent addition to their meals; but no one considered it of special interest until 1965. In that year a visiting zoologist noted that it was unlike any other small cat he knew and sent specimens to the National Science Museum in Tokyo. The Iriomote cat was soon declared to be not only a new species but the sole representative of an entirely new genus: *Mayailurus*.

Discoveries of new mammals have been rare events in recent years, so the new cat generated a huge amount of interest. The excitement has since turned to argument, however, since almost every scientist that examines the Iriomote cat has a different opinion of its status. Some still insist that it belongs in a genus of its own, while others maintain that it is no more than a local subspecies of the common leopard cat *Felis bengalensis*. A third body of opinion takes the middle ground and insists that the Iriomote is a cousin of the leopard cat from the genus *Prionailurus*.

Anatomically the Iriomote cat is similar to several Asian wildcats, but appearances can be deceptive. Usually the only reliable way to confirm true zoological relationships is by genetic analysis. However, in the

---

DATA PANEL

Iriomote cat

Mayailurus iriomotensis
(*Felis iriomotensis*,
***Prionailurus iriomotensis*)**

Family: Felidae

World population: Fewer than 100

Distribution: Only on Iriomote Island, Ryukyu (Nansei), Japan

Habitat: Lowland subtropical rain forest

Size: Length head/body: 19.5–23.5 in (50–60 cm); tail: 8 in (20 cm). Weight: 6.6–10 lb (3–4.5 kg)

Form: Short-legged cat with brown fur marked with rows of dark spots and 7 distinct lines on back of neck

Diet: Lizards and small mammals, including bats; occasionally frogs, crabs, and fish; also birds

Breeding: One to 4 kittens born April–May after gestation of 8–10 weeks. Life span up to 10 years in wild, 15 in captivity

Related endangered species: Flat-headed cat (*Prionailurus planiceps*) VU; bay cat (*Catopuma badia*) VU; also several big-cat species

Status: IUCN EN; CITES II

11   10   9   8

30   12

See also: What Is a Species? **1:** 26; The Animal Kingdom **1:** 58; Lynx, Iberian **6:** 52; Ocelot, Texas **7:** 20

The Iriomote cat *is similar in appearance to many Asian wildcats.*

Iriomote cat's case even DNA fingerprinting has proved inconclusive. The genetic evidence implies that the leopard and Iriomote cats became separate species only 200,000 years ago; yet fossil evidence on the island suggests that the cats of Iriomote were distinct as long as 2 million years ago.

The World's Rarest Feline?

The debate might seem academic, but the Iriomote cat's survival may depend on what the scientists eventually decide. Fewer than 100 individuals survive on an island measuring just 110 square miles (300 sq. km). If the cat is indeed a species in its own right, it is the world's rarest feline and worthy of a substantial conservation effort. As a subspecies of the common leopard cat, however, it would receive much less scientific and international support. Local people already see it as an obstacle to development on their small island home and would prefer that conservationists did not take an interest in it.

Since the discovery of the cat, a large area of Iriomote's hilly, sparsely inhabited interior has been declared a national park, and tourists have begun visiting. Unfortunately, however, the best habitat for the cats is not in the park but on the coastal lowlands, where conservation concerns inevitably run up against economic pressures. In the lowlands the cats are at risk from road traffic and habitat loss through land clearance for agriculture or tourist developments. They also face competition from domestic and stray cats living around the villages.

The Iriomote cat's predicament poses a dilemma. The population is tiny, although apparently quite stable, and the island on which it lives is so small that every patch of remaining habitat is important. The cats are highly territorial; so, given the limited space available, it is unlikely that their numbers would ever increase by much, even if all development on the island stopped. They have never been found anywhere else in the world, so moving them to other habitats would mean introducing nonnative predators into ecosystems where they do not belong. In the light of all these considerations it is not clear how the conflicting conservation demands can be resolved.

Stalking, pouncing, and killing prey *in 12 small-cat species. All of these cats are listed by CITES, and all are under review by the IUCN.*
1: *Ocelot* **2:** *Margay cat* **3:** *Tiger cat* **4:** *Jaguarundi* **5:** *European wildcat* **6:** *African wildcat* **7:** *Black-footed cat* **8:** *Sand cat* **9:** *Jungle cat* **10:** *Leopard cat* **11:** *Asiatic golden cat* **12:** *Fishing cat.*

1

2

7

6

5

4

3

Catfish, Giant

Pangasianodon gigas

Some of the smallest and largest freshwater fish known to science are catfish. Among the latter there is a toothless, vegetarian giant from the Mekong River—known as the giant catfish. The fish is both sacred and hunted, and its young have not been seen in the wild since the day the species was officially described in 1930.

For a species that has been fished regularly and whose migratory route is firmly established, remarkably little is known about the biology of the giant catfish. Even the validity of its scientific name is in doubt, leading to uncertainty about the true identity of the fish. Some studies indicate that the giant catfish may be better placed in a bigger group: the genus *Pangasius* that contains its closest relatives.

Since numbers of giant catfish in the wild are believed to be small, it could be some time before the situation is resolved. Answers to some of the outstanding questions about the giant catfish's biology and life stages may be provided by studies of captive-bred stocks that are currently being raised for reintroduction into some of the giant catfish's traditional waters.

Search for Clues

The giant catfish—along with its 20 or so *Pangasius* relatives—belongs to the shark catfish family (Pangasiidae). All family members have an elongated body form, a distinctive dorsal (back) fin, an underslung mouth, undulating swimming movements, and an overall passing resemblance in body shape to the true sharks. The Pangasiidae are also closely related to the glass or schilbeid catfish family (Schilbeidae). Some authorities believe that they should each be regarded as a subfamily of a single family rather than as two separate families.

There are two features that set the giant catfish apart from its nearest relatives: the absence of barbels (whiskers) on the lower jaw and the lack of teeth.

However, these features—which are characteristic of adult specimens—may be less evident in juveniles, or may only relate to the adult phase of the species.

It has been observed that in some *Pangasius* species teeth gradually disappear with age. It is possible that the same applies to the giant catfish, but since no small or even medium-sized specimens have ever been collected or observed in the wild, the theory is unproven. It has also been proposed that the barbels may

DATA PANEL

Giant catfish (Mekong catfish, Thailand giant catfish)

Pangasianodon gigas

Family: Pangasiidae

World population: Low, but exact numbers unknown

Distribution: Mekong River system through Cambodia, Laos, Thailand, Vietnam, and (possibly) part of China

Habitat: Major watercourses and lakes

Size: Length: 6.6–9.8 ft (2–3 m). Weight: 240–660 lb (110–300 kg)

Form: Dorsal (back) profile almost straight; curved belly; flattened head. Lower jaw barbels (whiskers) absent. Large eyes set low on head. Both dorsal and pectoral (chest) fins have prominent spines along front edge; caudal (tail) fin is powerful and forked

Diet: Vegetarian: algae and soft, succulent plants

Breeding: Migrates up to several thousand miles upriver between mid-April and end of May, possibly as far north as Lake Tali in Yunnan, China. Induced spawning in captive-bred specimens has yielded on average 17.6–22 lb (8–10 kg) of eggs

Related endangered species: No close relatives, but Barnard's rock catfish (*Austroglanis barnardi*), in the same order of fish, is Critically Endangered

Status: IUCN EN; CITES I

See also: Research **1:** 84; Cultural Differences **1:** 94; Totoaba **9:** 92

be present even in adult specimens, but that they are overgrown by flesh as the jaws become progressively fatter with advancing age. To establish whether or not barbels are present at some stage in the giant catfish's life, juvenile specimens, as well as a series of progressively older ones, would have to be examined.

Threats to Survival

Since so little is known about the life of the giant catfish, it is impossible to say with any certainty what influence environmental factors have had, or are having, on wild populations. However, it is known that intense fishing over many years brought the species to the brink of extinction. The present situation may be a little more hopeful, particularly after the release of some 20,000 young fish from recently established captive-breeding programs into rivers previously inhabited by giant catfish. It is hoped that the captive-bred fish will become established and help sustain the fisheries that exist.

One of the local fisheries has traditionally been associated with Thai New Year festivities during April and May. Coincidentally, it is then that the flesh of the giant catfish is at its tastiest, since the fish have used up much of their body fat during their upstream spawning migration.

Perhaps even more important than the actual flavor of the flesh is the belief that eating giant catfish —or *pla buek* as it is known locally—leads to a long, healthy, and prosperous life. Add together the two "ingredients" of excellent taste and life-enhancing qualities, and it is easy to understand why the giant catfish commands a high price in Thailand.

Giant catfish have also been fished over the years for oil extraction. Large fish—which can weigh well over 220 pounds (100 kg)—yield correspondingly large quantities of oil. Oil extraction is therefore a worthwhile exercise, despite the fact that wild population levels are low and that fist-sized stones, sometimes found in the stomachs of the giant catfish (perhaps swallowed while feeding on algae-covered rock), wreak havoc with oil-extraction machinery.

An expanding database of information relating to the giant catfish is now emerging. As more is learned about the fish's biology and lifestyle, there will be a greater understanding of how best to conserve the species: Conservationists can use the available data to plan effective strategies for the fish's protection. As current efforts begin to take effect—they include the release of captive-bred specimens and controlled fishing by various fisheries—the fortunes of the giant catfish could be about to take a turn for the better.

The giant catfish *belongs to the shark catfish family and is not unlike a true shark in body shape. The absence of whiskers and teeth in adults distinguishes it from its nearest relatives.*

Cavefish, Alabama

Speoplatyrhinus poulsoni

There are probably only about 100 Alabama cavefish alive today. Such a low number makes the species not just the rarest fish known to science, but also one of the most endangered vertebrates on the planet, teetering between survival and extinction.

The Alabama cavefish is known from just one site: Key Cave on the northern bank of the Tennessee River in Alabama, on the edge of the man-made Pickwick Lake. While the Alabama cavefish may in the past have been more widely distributed, searches carried out in other subterranean waters in the region have failed to yield any specimens. Furthermore, other caves that may have been potential habitats for the cavefish were flooded when Pickwick Lake was created.

As in most caves of any size, conditions within Key Cave remain fairly constant throughout the year, and the animals that live there form an interdependent ecological unit. The cave itself is large and has several levels. In total, some 10,000 feet (3,000 m) of passages have been mapped. The two entrances along Pickwick Lake are major points of entry and exit to a population of gray bats and other organisms, while permanent Key Cave residents include copepods, amphipods, and isopods (all small crustaceans), as well as some larger crustacea, including three species of crayfish.

Little-Known Species

The Alabama cavefish remains little known because of its extremely low numbers, not just in the wild but in museums as well. There are only nine specimens in collections, and none has, to date, been dissected for gut-content analysis. Cave visits have also yielded little in the way of concrete biological data, since the maximum number of individuals ever observed has never exceeded 10. Much about the cavefish's biology therefore has to be inferred, either from what is known of conditions in Key Cave or from the biology of other, better-known cavefish species.

For example, the Ozark cavefish is known to feed on its own young, and by extrapolation it is thought that the Alabama cavefish may do the same. If this is

---

DATA PANEL

Alabama cavefish

Speoplatyrhinus poulsoni

Family: Amblyopsidae

World population: Probably as low as 100

Distribution: Key Cave on the Tennessee River in Lauderdale County, Alabama

Habitat: Cool-water alkaline pools

Size: Length: 2.8 in (7.2 cm) is the maximum recorded, but larger specimens seen in cave

Form: Eyeless, elongated, pink-bodied fish with flattened head and snout. The head is a third of the body length. Unusually, the anal opening, or vent, is situated forward in throat region. Highly developed lateral line; also sensory papillae on the caudal peduncle (base of tail fin) and along the top and bottom rays of the caudal (tail) fin

Diet: Small aquatic invertebrates, including young crayfish and (possibly) its own offspring

Breeding: Poorly known. Probably fewer than 10% of females breed in any given year. Few eggs are produced, and they, along with the newly hatched larvae, are believed to be incubated within the gill chamber

Related endangered species: Ozark cavefish (*Amblyopsis rosae*) VU; northern cavefish (*A. spelaea*) VU; southern cavefish (*Typhlichthys subterraneus*) VU

Status: IUCN CR; not listed by CITES

See also: Organizations **1:** 10; Captive Breeding **1:** 87; Archerfish, Western **2:** 28; Characin, Blind Cave **3:** 38; Rocky, Eastern Province **8:** 40

the case, it could offer at least a partial explanation for its low numbers. It is also assumed that the copepods, amphipods, and isopods that inhabit the cave form the other major dietary items, possibly along with juvenile crayfish.

In terms of reproductive strategy the Alabama cavefish may be a gill-chamber brooder, meaning that it may incubate its eggs within a specially enlarged part of the gill chamber. The northern cavefish is known to exhibit such behavior, protecting both its eggs and newly hatched larvae within its similarly adapted gill chambers.

Threats and Recovery

Some of the threats facing the Alabama cavefish are clearcut, the most obvious being its restricted distribution and small population. A less direct but equally important threat comes from the decline of Key Cave's gray bat population. Studies carried out on fish populations in other caves have shown that as the bat populations have declined, so have populations of some other species, most notably those of the southern cavefish. Even though the cavefish does not actually feed on the bats or their droppings, they do rely on aquatic invertebrates that benefit from bat guano (dung).

The existence of the southern cavefish in several caves close to the Alabama cavefish's habitat could also pose a serious threat; indeed, it is possible that

The Alabama cavefish lives in a single cave system on the banks of the Tennessee River. It has no eyes; instead, it senses its way around its dark, subterranean enviroment.

the southern cavefish may have led to the disappearance of the Alabama cavefish, although no proof has ever come to light. Predation by large crayfish may also present a danger; one species found in Key Cave has been seen to prey on the southern cavefish. Another danger could be groundwater pollution from the surrounding areas, and particularly seepage of chemicals from crop treatments or from a sewage-disposal facility in the nearby city of Florence.

To protect the fish, the Tennessee Valley Authority has fenced off the two entrances to the cave. In addition, constant monitoring of water quality in the region will give rapid warning of any impending crises. If forest, crop, and water-management plans are properly observed, a number of major threats to Key Cave may be averted. Just as important, however, is preserving the health of the gray bat population, which seems to have recovered from a decline of nearly 50 percent between 1969 and 1970.

If all the potential threats are kept in check, the Alabama cavefish may survive. In the meantime, however, a thorough search needs to be put into place in other caves in the region in an attempt to find other, as yet undiscovered populations of this endangered species.

Chameleon, South Central Lesser

Furcifer minor

A striking reptile, the south central lesser chameleon tends to inhabit small, scattered areas in the southern part of central Madagascar, an island republic off the east coast of Africa. It was not well known until reptile exports from Madagascar began to increase in the late 1980s. Its relative scarcity and limited distribution make it vulnerable to threats such as collecting and habitat loss.

Until recently the south central lesser chameleon species was simply referred to by its scientific (Latin) name: *Furcifer minor*. American reptile keepers coined the common name—south central lesser chameleon—to reflect both its geographical distribution and the second part of its scientific name: *minor*, or lesser.

Color Changes

It would be easy to assume that the male and female of the lesser chameleon belonged to two different species; males are much larger than females, their coloration is different, and the male sports two rostral processes (hornlike projections) on his snout. As with all chameleons, they can change color but do not (contrary to popular belief) simply change to match their surroundings. All chameleons are already well camouflaged, and color change is activated by temperature and mood. When cool, the chameleon gets darker, so it absorbs heat. When faced with a threat, the color and the pattern change; males of certain species can exhibit brilliant colors. Male color change or intensification is also visible during courtship. Females that have mated or do not wish to mate usually signal this by changes in color or pattern.

The lesser chameleon is unusual in that the female exhibits a stunning combination of green, black, yellow, and red, with two violet-blue spots on each side of the body. The bright red is mainly on top of the head and in the folds of the gular (throat) pouch. Males are also striking, the two processes with their jagged edges giving them a somewhat primitive appearance. Both sexes have a dorsal crest of spines and a casque (helmetlike structure) at the back of the head. Both features are slightly more pronounced in the males.

The exact population size and distribution of the south central lesser chameleon are not known precisely. The lizard has been observed mainly in scattered locations in the southern part of the central domain of Madagascar. Although not known to adapt to altered habitat, there has been a report of the species being found in a coffee plantation. The central domain is mainly a plateau with hills and valleys where conditions are cooler and

DATA PANEL

South central lesser chameleon

Furcifer minor

Family: Chamaeleonidae

World population: Unknown

Distribution: Southern part of the central plateau, Madagascar

Habitat: Remaining areas of original dry savanna forests

Size: Length head/body: male up to 9 in (23.7 cm); female up to 6 in (15.7 cm)

Form: Male is light to reddish brown with scattered darker brown patches and a few diagonal light bands on the body. The anterior part of the body carries a brown-edged white stripe or 2 spots on each side. Female is light green, but 2 violet spots and a few yellowish streaks are often present

Diet: Insects

Breeding: Clutch of 11–16 eggs; 2–3 clutches per year. Eggs are buried in soft soil and leaf litter; incubation period of 9–10 months

Related endangered species: Labord's chameleon (*Furcifer labordi*) VU; Madagascar forest chameleon (*F. campani*) VU

Status: IUCN VU; CITES II

TANZANIA
COMOROS
MALAWI
MADAGASCAR
MOZAMBIQUE

See also: Speciation 1: 26; Iguana, Galápagos Land 5: 76

rainfall is lower than in the east domain. Reports that the lesser chameleon has been found in another part of the country need verification.

Problems facing the lesser chameleon are common to many animal and plant species in Madagascar, one of the poorest countries in the world. The chameleon's IUCN listing is based on reduction of numbers, habitat loss, and possible threats from exploitation such as collecting for sale. Land clearance for agriculture and overgrazing by cattle have also denuded many areas, causing soil erosion and habitat destruction.

Protection

Wildlife has been protected on Madagascar since 1881, and some of the first reserves in the world were established there as early as 1927. Over the past few decades conservation on Madagascar has been targeted by various international

organizations, and national parks and reserves have been established. Protection is not guaranteed; unless Madagascar's economy improves, people will continue to clear the land to make a living. The few cents earned by selling a lizard to a dealer are often desperately needed.

In 1995 the CITES committee suspended the export of all but four species of Madagascar's chameleons. In 1999, to help make monitoring easier, only three exporters were granted licenses to trade, and annual quotas were set for each of the four species. The ban will continue until it can be proved that trade will not deplete numbers. If the ban stays, the south central lesser chameleon, with its fairly high reproductive rate, may survive. However, its future also depends on protection of its habitat. A few specimens are held in captivity, but captive breeding is not always successful.

Male and female *south central lesser chameleons have strikingly different coloration. The male (above) is reddish brown and up to 3 inches (7.8 cm) longer than the light-green female (right).*

Characin, Blind Cave

Astyanax mexicanus

The blind cave characin is now known to be the same, genetically, as the Mexican tetra. Isolated in three separate cave systems, the fish is vulnerable to many threats.

In 1949 a pink, eyeless fish was imported into Europe. It immediately caused a stir among public aquarium visitors and aquarium keepers. Despite its apparent disability, the fish could find food just as easily as its sighted counterparts. Within a short time it had become popular all over the world. The initial burst of enthusiasm has now diminished, but the blind cave characin continues to attract attention whenever it is exhibited.

Nonidentical Twins

No one could have guessed at the time that the blind cave characin was the same, genetically, as another fish known as the Mexican tetra. At first sight the two fish look so different that they could belong to two distinct species or even, possibly, genera. Yet on closer inspection the underlying similarities soon become apparent. If you ignore the silver, black, and other colors on a Mexican tetra, you end up with a pink fish. Now imagine some fatty tissue over each eye, and the Mexican tetra is transformed into the blind cave characin.

In genetic terms such dramatic differences in appearance can be brought about by relatively minor changes, or mutations, over many generations. The changes are created by being subjected—through natural selection—to the evolutionary pressures of living in caves under conditions of permanent darkness. Studies of genetic material (DNA) carried out on populations of Mexican tetra, both cave or hypogean (those that live belowground) and normal or epigean (those that live aboveground), have confirmed that the Mexican tetra and blind cave characin belong to the same species.

Further proof, if it were needed, occurs in at least one cave in Mexico—Cueva Chica. Periodically, colored and fully sighted Mexican tetras are flushed into the cave when a nearby river floods. Here, in the darkness, they interbreed with their cave counterparts, totally oblivious of their color and eye differences, but able to

DATA PANEL

Blind cave characin (sardina ciega)

Astyanax mexicanus

Family: Characidae

World population: Unknown

Distribution: Mexico, including caves in the Sierras del Abra, de Guatemala, de Perez, and de Colmena

Habitat: Freshwater pools in limestone caves

Size: Length: 3.5 in (9 cm)

Form: Pink, eyeless fish; reduced scales; anal fin is completely straight in females but convex in males

Diet: Wide-ranging; includes bat droppings, other fish, and eggs

Breeding: Slightly adhesive eggs are scattered over substratum and abandoned (parents may consume own eggs). Hatching takes about 1 day at about 75°F (24°C); may

take up to 3 days at lower temperatures; newborn fish (fry) become free-swimming 3 days later

Related endangered species: None, but some epigean (aboveground) populations of *Astyanaz mexicanus* are known to be declining. In the same family the naked characin (*Gymnocharacinus bergii*) of Argentina is Endangered

Status: IUCN VU; not listed by CITES

See also: What Is a Species? **1:** 26; Inbreeding Blind Interbreeding **1:** 56; Cavefish, Alabama **3:** 34; Goodeid, Gold Sawfin **5:** 36

respond to all the other cues that identify each to the other as belonging to one and the same species.

Records of interbreeding between river and cave populations were being made as far back as 1942, but it took many years for the knowledge to become accepted universally. Even then, two different scientific names persisted until constant repetition brought the necessary shift toward uniformity.

Lurking Threats

The blind cave characin has a restricted distribution and is native to just three main cave systems. The caves are completely separated from each other, which means that populations are isolated. Hence the status of the cave populations is clearly of concern. In such diverse and complicated water systems the threat of pollution can never be totally discounted. Neither can the effects of extended droughts in the region, which can result in dangerous lowering of water levels in the pools inhabited by the cave fish. Pumping of the cave water for irrigation purposes also lowers water levels. In addition, more widespread hybridization between the aboveground and belowground types could lead to a dilution of "cave characteristics" in at least some populations.

Overall, the future of the blind cave characin is insecure. Any of the above factors—all of which are avoidable—could in a short time render the fish Critically Endangered or Extinct in its native habitat. A drop in water level would be one of the quickest routes to extinction. In the event of such a disaster fish bred commercially for the aquarium trade could be used to replace the wild communities, but only if their native habitats were deemed suitable for restocking.

The blind cave characin *lacks any body pigment and has only fat-covered, vestigal eyes, unlike the Mexican tetra (inset). Despite looking completely different and living in separate habitats, the two are genetically almost identical.*

Cheetah

Acinonyx jubatus

The cheetah is well known for its lean body, great speed, and spotted coat. Years of persecution have made it one of the world's most vulnerable big cats.

The world's fastest land animal over short distances, the cheetah is also the most ancient of all the big cats. Cheetahs probably evolved on the plains of the Middle East four million years ago. Fossil evidence shows that 10,000 years ago cheetahs roamed in places as far apart as North America, Europe, Asia, and Africa. The cheetah's heyday lasted until the last ice age; since then human populations have exploded, and the cheetah's range and numbers have shrunk. In their ancestral homeland of the Middle East the Asian subspecies of cheetah is critically endangered, with very few, if any, animals left in remote parts of Iran and Afghanistan. The situation is only slightly better in Africa.

Cheetahs differ from other big cats in their adaptations for hunting. The shape of a cheetah—a narrow, elongated body and long, muscular legs—is ideal for sprinting. Unlike its cousins, the cheetah cannot completely retract its claws; it needs them to provide extra grip when running at high speeds. Cheetahs take advantage of the fact that other large predators rest during the hottest part of the day and do their hunting in the late morning and early afternoon. A cheetah first stalks its prey, then runs it down at speeds of up to 60 miles per hour (95 km/h). The flexibility of the cat's long spine allows it to take huge strides. Most chases are over in about 20 seconds—any prey that can evade capture for more than a minute will probably escape since the cheetah cannot maintain its speed for long.

Cheetahs kill by clamping their jaws around the victim's throat. This has the effect of closing off the windpipe, so the prey stops breathing. The cheetah does not have particularly big teeth, but exceptionally large nostrils ensure that, even when out of breath from the chase, it can inhale deeply through its nose while maintaining a suffocating grip with its jaws.

DATA PANEL

Cheetah

Acinonyx jubatus

Family: Felidae

World population: 2,000–15,000

Distribution: Sub-Saharan Africa, excluding Congo Basin; most of South Africa

Habitat: Grasslands

Size: Length head/body: 44–60 in (112–152 cm); tail: 20–33 in (51–84 cm); height at shoulder: 25–37 in (64–94 cm); males slightly larger than females. Weight: 86–143 lb (39–65 kg)

Form: Slender big cat with long, muscular legs, small head, and long, curved tail. Coat golden yellow with black spots; small, rounded ears; black stripes either side of nose

Diet: Mainly gazelles; also impala, warthogs, small antelopes, gamebirds, and hares

Breeding: Between 1 and 8 young (average 3–5) born at any time of year (peak births March–June). Life span 12–14 years in the wild; up to 17 years in captivity

Related endangered species: No close relatives

Status: IUCN VU; CITES I

40

See also: Genetics 1: 56; Jaguar 5: 86; Leopard 6: 28; Leopard, Clouded 6: 30

Cheetah means "spotted one" in Hindi, and every cheetah has markings as unique as a fingerprint. In some Zimbabwean cheetahs the

A cheetah *can achieve speeds of 0 to 45 miles per hour (0 to 72 km/h) in 2.5 seconds—acceleration to rival some sports cars.*

spots along the back and tail join up to form a blotchy pattern. Animals with this distinctive pattern are called king cheetahs and they were once thought to be a separate subspecies. However, it has been shown that they are simply part of the natural variation within the local population. The black "tear stripes" on the cheetah's face are thought to help protect their eyes from sunlight reflecting off their cheeks. Human athletes imitate this idea when they daub paint across their cheeks and noses.

Cheetahs breed at any time of year. A female is in heat and ready to mate every 12 days unless she already has cubs. She will give birth to three to five cubs per litter; but infant mortality is high, and fewer than one-third of all cubs survive to adulthood. Small, widely scattered cheetah populations mean that much inbreeding occurs, and many cubs are born with genetic defects. A solution might be to release some animals from captivity, bringing in fresh genetic stock.

Tourist Attraction

Cheetahs face problems even in protected national parks. Tourists want to see the cheetahs wherever possible, and this tends to scare off prey and distracts the animals from hunting. Disturbance of cheetah kills also allows scavengers such as jackals to nip in and steal the food. Cheetahs are not good at defending themselves from this sort of interference.

Chimpanzee

Pan troglodytes

Despite its protected status, a shrinking habitat and continued poaching are major problems facing Africa's "common" chimpanzee, and populations are rapidly dying out.

Throughout central Africa human populations are expanding, and there is a growing pressure on the land from people trying to make a living. In many areas everyday human practices are putting chimpanzees at risk. Despite the fact that this animal is a close relative—we share 98 percent of our genes with chimps—it receives little sympathy when it becomes a competitor for space.

Although wild chimpanzees are protected by law in several African countries, regulations are difficult to enforce, especially in areas of central Africa torn apart by political instability and civil war. Moreover, legal protection does not include protection of their habitat.

The tropical forests, already reduced to a fraction of their original size, continue to be logged and cleared for agriculture. The remaining areas are often so disturbed by people hunting, collecting firewood, or herding their livestock that the chimpanzee population moves on or dies out. Today wild chimpanzees live in isolated patches of habitat, some of which are too small to support a healthy, viable population. As a result, levels of inbreeding increase, leading to genetic problems and birth defects.

Nevertheless, in some areas the chimpanzees are traditionally tolerated and respected, even to the extent that they are allowed to wander into crop fields and village markets. Local people do no more than "shoo" them away if they become a nuisance.

Chimpanzees *are stocky, powerful animals that use a combination of brainpower and brawn to survive in a variety of habitats, including rain forests, deciduous forests, and swamp forests. They are even capable of making and using tools.*

DATA PANEL

Chimpanzee (common chimpanzee)

Pan troglodytes

Family: Pongidae

World population: Unknown, but might exceed 150,000

Distribution: Tropical western and central Africa, from Senegal and Angola to Tanzania and Sudan

Habitat: Rain forest, deciduous forest, swamp forest, and savanna grassland with access to evergreen fruiting trees

Size: Length: 28–38 in (71–97 cm); height at shoulder: 39–66 in (95–165 cm); males slightly larger than females. Weight: 66–110 lb (30–50 kg)

Form: Large ape covered in long, brown-black hair. Palms and face are bare; adults are sometimes bald. Skin on face is wrinkled, usually pink or brown, darkening with age. Projecting jaw has large, expressive lips

Diet: Fruit, leaves; also seeds, shoots, bark, flowers, honey, and insects; some meat from smaller animals, including monkeys and wild pigs

Breeding: Single young born at any time of year after gestation of 7–8 months; weaned at 3–4 years; stays with mother until mature at 7 years. Life span may exceed 35 years

Related endangered species: Gorilla *(Gorilla gorilla)* EN; orang-utan *(Pongo pygmaeus)** EN; pygmy chimpanzee *(Pan paniscus)** EN

Status: IUCN EN; CITES I

See also: Populations **1:** 20; Exploitation of Live Animals **1:** 49; Chimpanzee, Pygmy **3:** 44

However, this kind of tolerance is the exception to the rule: In other parts of their range chimpanzees are treated as pests and killed to protect crops. Some are caught in snares or shot and eaten as bush meat. Their body parts have also been used in traditional medicines and rituals. Perhaps most disturbing of all, chimpanzees are captured live and sold as pets or for medical research. This trade represents a huge loss of life; for every young chimp that reaches its final destination, several more will have died in transit. The young chimps' mothers are often also killed in the poachers' efforts to kidnap the baby.

A Captive Future

There are large numbers of chimpanzees in captivity all around the world. Many are kept as illegal pets or held in unlicensed collections, but a great number are in zoos and conservation centers. Of those born and bred in captivity, some are of mixed race, with parents from different regions of Africa who would never normally have met in the wild. It is unlikely that any of these captive-raised chimpanzees will be successfully returned to the wild. Like human babies, young chimpanzees are born with few

instincts and must learn from their elders the skills they need to survive. Individuals born in captivity have often been hand-reared by keepers and are therefore ill-equipped for life in the wild. They are also likely to have difficulty in rearing their own young. In addition, captive chimpanzees may carry diseases that could destroy a wild population.

There is more hope for wild-born chimpanzees that have been rescued from illegal collections. Animals such as these can be taken to one of several rehabilitation centers in Africa where they can practice their "wild" skills in large enclosures before being set free. However, releases are still risky. The danger of disease, or of chimpanzees being attacked by established populations, means that they are usually released in areas from which the species has already disappeared.

Chimpanzee, Pygmy

Pan paniscus

The pygmy chimpanzee, or bonobo, is less well known than its cousin the common chimpanzee, but it faces a familiar combination of problems. Habitat destruction and illegal poaching rank high on the list of threats that must be addressed if the species is to survive.

Pygmy and common chimpanzees are so similar that the pygmy—or bonobo—was not recognized as a separate species until 1929. This was partly because of the bonobo's rather limited geographical range. Bonobos are found only in the remote dense forest south of the Zaire River in Africa. For this reason they have remained relatively undisturbed while hundreds of their common cousins were captured for zoos, museums, and other collections throughout the last 200 years. People have only started to kill bonobos quite recently. Populations are now so heavily poached that radical conservation measures are urgently needed if the species is to escape extinction.

The pygmy chimpanzee is protected, and international trade in living and dead specimens is subject to the most stringent regulations. However, animals are still used in medical research, and this demand sustains a black market in their trade.

Although there has been extensive research on the lives of chimpanzees, relatively little is known about bonobos in the wild. They usually live in large social groups, or troops, with between 50 and 120 members. Within each group there are smaller subgroups, usually centered on an older female and her offspring. Newborn chimpanzees are as helpless as human babies—although they mature a lot faster—and each youngster needs up to seven years of individual care and attention from its mother. Male chimpanzees usually remain close to their mother into adulthood, and their status in the group depends on the rank of their mother. Young females, on the other hand, usually move on to join another troop before they mate, which helps to avoid inbreeding.

Bonobos form closer relationships with each other than common chimpanzees do. The bonds between males and females and between individuals of the same sex are reinforced with sessions of mutual grooming in which the chimps pick parasites and debris from each other's fur. Common chimpanzees groom each other too, but it is usually lower-ranking males appeasing their high-ranking seniors.

DATA PANEL

Pygmy chimpanzee (dwarf chimpanzee, bonobo)

Pan paniscus

Family: Pongidae

World population: Unknown; maybe about 15,000

Distribution: South of Zaire River in central Africa

Habitat: Lowland and swamp forests alongside Zaire River

Size: Length: 28–33 in (70–83 cm); males up to 30% bigger than females. Weight: 68–86 lb (31–39 kg)

Form: Similar to common chimpanzee, although slightly less robust, with longer legs and smaller molar teeth; facial skin is dark

Diet: Mostly plant material, including fruit, leaves, shoots, seeds, flowers, pith, and bark; some animal matter, including ants, termites, worms and other invertebrates, small mammals, and snakes

Breeding: Single young born at any time of year after gestation of 7–8 months; stays with mother until mature at about 7 years. Life span unknown, but could be 20 years

Related endangered species: Chimpanzee *(Pan troglodytes)** EN; gorilla *(Gorilla gorilla)* EN; orang-utan *(Pongo pygmaeus)** EN

Status: IUCN EN; CITES I

See also: Speciation 1: 26; Chimpanzee 3: 42

The pygmy chimpanzee

is leaner than the common chimpanzee, but not really any smaller. The skin on the face is dark, even in young animals, and the hair on the head tends to grow in tufts that stick out to the sides behind the ears.

Pressure on Habitat

Loss of habitat has had a direct effect on the bonobo's existence. When too many individuals occupy an area, competition for food between neighboring troops intensifies, causing increased aggression. The birthrate usually drops as stress levels rise, and any young that are born will suffer with the rest from food shortages. Conflict between troops is another source of disturbance to bonobo populations.

Encroaching human settlements are also affecting the bonobo's habitat. The timber industry is responsible for bringing large numbers of people to the forests to work in tree felling. Some of them stay, attempting to make a living from farming the degraded soil. As a result, impoverished communities have sprung up all over Africa in the wake of timber extraction, and the region's wildlife is severely threatened by such disturbance. Not only do animals come into conflict with farmers trying to eke out a living, they also provide a tempting source of illegal but lucrative income. The deteriorating economic situation in the Democratic Republic of Congo (formerly Zaire) in the 1990s, along with wars in the region, have also hampered wildlife conservation.

Chinchilla, Short-Tailed

Chinchilla brevicaudata

The short-tailed chinchilla has not been seen in the wild for almost 50 years. The future of any surviving populations almost certainly depends on who finds them first—conservationists or fur trappers.

The short-tailed chinchilla is a rabbit-sized, mostly nocturnal animal. In many ways it is a typical rodent. It lives in burrows or rock crevices in a fairly secure habitat of mountain slopes and is capable of breeding two or three times a year. If disturbed, it retreats quickly into its burrow, but will emerge again seconds later to double check that the danger has passed.

Anyone wondering why the species is so critically endangered needs only to touch the animal's bluish-gray coat. Chinchillas have what is widely considered the softest and finest fur of any mammal. It has been highly prized by people since the Incas, South American Indians who ruled an empire based on Peru from the 12th century. The Incas mostly hunted chinchillas for their meat.

The chinchilla's extremely fine fur is an essential adaptation to life at high altitudes; the animal lives at higher altitudes than almost any other mammal. The nights are intensely cold, and any warm-blooded creature needs effective insulation in order to survive. Like bird down, chinchilla fur is warm and soft when dry, but deteriorates quickly if it gets damp. To keep its fur in good condition, the chinchilla grooms frequently; it also grows a new coat during the molting season. However, once the animal has been killed and skinned, the fur must be kept dry to be of any use. The Incas—who had limited use for such delicate fur—kept hunting at fairly low levels. However, when Europeans settled in the region after the Spanish conquest of 1532, they showed no restraint. At that time it was usual to find chinchillas living in colonies of over 100 animals, and they could be seen hopping around at dawn and dusk or basking in the sun outside their burrows. Commercial chinchilla hunting began in 1828. By using far more sophisticated trapping techniques than had been available before, the hunters caught more animals.

DATA PANEL

Short-tailed chinchilla

Chinchilla brevicaudata

Family: Chinchillidae

World population: Unknown; possibly extinct in the wild

Distribution: Northern Argentina, Bolivia, northern Chile, and southern Peru

Habitat: Rocky mountain slopes at 9,800–16,400 ft (3,000–5,000 m) above sea level

Size: Length head/body: 8.5–15 in (22–38 cm); tail: 2.7–5.8 in (7–15 cm); female up to 80% larger than male. Weight: 14–28 oz (400–800 g)

Form: Rabbit-sized, bushy-tailed rodent with incredibly dense, silky-soft gray fur; tail has a dark streak along its length. Large black eyes, and large rounded ears

Diet: Almost any plant material: seeds, fruit, grain, herbs, and mosses

Breeding: Two or 3 litters of 1–6 (usually 1 or 2) young born May–November after 4-month gestation; weaned at 6 weeks; mature at about 8 months. Life span up to 10 years in the wild

Related endangered species: Long-tailed chinchilla (*Chinchilla lanigera*) VU

Status: IUCN CR; CITES I

See also: What Is an Endangered Species? **1:** 8; Luxury Products **1:** 46; Beaver, Eurasian **2:** 76; Antelope, Tibetan **2:** 26

The demand for chinchilla fur from the fashion centers of Europe and North America was insatiable. It took over 400 chinchillas to make one luxury coat, which could be sold for up to $100,000. The demand made chinchilla fur, weight for weight, the most valuable in the world. Records show that in the early 1900s Chile alone was exporting over half a million chinchilla skins a year to Britain, France, Germany, and the United States. The actual death toll would have been far higher: Some skins would have been damaged or used domestically, and probably many more animals were trapped and sold illegally. The figures include both short-tailed and common chinchillas, but the short-tailed variety was thought to have the finest fur and, being slightly larger than its cousin, was especially valuable.

Protection Measures

By 1910 chinchilla populations had fallen so low that the four countries in which the animals lived— Argentina, Bolivia, Chile, and Peru—signed a treaty banning all chinchilla trapping. Inevitably, because of the remoteness of much of the chinchilla's habitat, however, the ban proved impossible to enforce. Instead, it had the effect of pushing up the price of black-market skins. A few years later, however, wild chinchillas were so rare that even illegal trapping became unprofitable.

Only at this point did the potential for farming chinchillas emerge, and today there are millions of chinchillas living in captivity on fur farms or as pets. Most captive populations are descended from a few wild-caught chinchillas introduced to the United States in 1923. Attempts to release chinchillas into the wild have failed so far; animals whose survival instincts have been dulled and diluted by generations of domestication do not generally fare well in the wild.

Uncertain Future

The last confirmed sighting of short-tailed chinchillas in the wild was in 1953, although there were reports of some living in Lauca National Park in Chile in 1970. Generally, a 30-year absence of sightings is fairly strong evidence that the species is extinct in the wild. However, the IUCN takes the view that while there are still areas of little-explored habitat in the region, some populations may survive undiscovered in the most remote and inaccessible parts of their range.

Chinchilla fur is incredibly dense and soft. It is also loosely attached; a predator trying to grab the chinchilla may be left with nothing but a mouthful of unappetizing fluff!

Cichlids, Lake Victoria Haplochromine

Haplochromis spp.

Restricted by nature to a certain habitat, many animal and plant species will often evolve into several types, each finely tuned by natural selection to fill every possible niche with little or no overlap. Such "species flocks" are able to survive side by side without much competition for space or food. This is the situation in the Great Rift lakes of Africa.

Africa's three major lakes, or "inland seas"—Lakes Malawi, Tanganyika, and Victoria—contain a bewildering array of fish species so diverse and colorful that they are often compared with coral reef fish. Each lake has its own endemic species (species found nowhere else). Lake Malawi is famous for *Aulonocara*, *Melanochromis*, and *Pseudotropheus* species, while Lake Tanganyika has *Lamprologus*, *Neolamprologus*, and *Julidochromis* species. Lake Victoria is renowned for haplochromine cichlids.

Lake Victoria

Lake Victoria is a massive body of fresh water. In surface dimensions it is the third largest lake in the world after Lake Superior and the Caspian Sea. It is, however, relatively shallow; its maximum depth is only 260 feet (80 m). Owing to its highly irregular coast profile, its shoreline is about 2,200 miles (3,500 km) long. Despite its colossal size, it is surrounded by land and is virtually cut off from major external influences. As a result, it has developed its own special characteristics, including hard and alkaline water.

Victoria Cichlids

Within this special environment habitats vary across the thousands of bays and inlets along the lake coastline, where a large number of fish species can be found. Estimates vary, but over 200—and probably closer to 400—endemic species of cichlids have evolved. More than half belong to the genus *Haplochromis*. Owing to the relative "youth" of Lake Victoria, the evolution of so many different cichlid species in such a short time has been referred to as an example of "explosive radiation," or "evolutionary avalanche."

Catastrophic Developments

A series of developments has affected these haplochromine populations. For example, pressures were created by a fast-expanding human population around the lake, and greater demand for arable land has resulted in forested areas

---

DATA PANEL

Lake Victoria haplochromine cichlids

**Haplochromis* spp.*

Family: Cichlidae

World population: Some 200 species are known to have become extinct since mid-1950s; population levels of remaining species are estimated to have decreased from about 80% of total biomass of the lake to about 1%

Distribution: Lake Victoria, East Africa

Habitat: Wide range of habitats mostly close to the lake bottom and in relatively shallow water

Size: Length: about 4 in (10 cm)

Form: Most species have laterally compressed bodies, large eyes and mouths, and well-formed fins. Dorsal (back) fin has spinous front half and soft-rayed back half. Males of most species exhibit egglike spots (egg dummies) on anal (belly) fin

Diet: Diverse, but specific to each species. Phytoplankton and zooplankton encrusting algae, insects, mollusks, crustaceans, eggs, larvae, or even scales of other fish

Breeding: Female lays small number of eggs (sometimes only 5, depending on size and species). Males stimulated to release sperm by females pecking at egg dummies. Eggs and sperm brooded orally by females; female guards young, taking them back into mouth if danger threatens

Related endangered species: All species of haplochromine in Lake Victoria

Status: Not individually listed by IUCN because too many, but *Haplochromis obliquidens*, for example, is EN; not listed by CITES

See also: Speciation **1:** 26; Introductions **1:** 54; Caracolera, Mojarra **3:** 26

The emerald-backed cichlid *(above) may be prey to the voracious Nile perch (below right) that was introduced to Lake Victoria in the 1950s.*

being cleared. This has led to increased runoff into the lake—both physical (silt) and chemical (fertilizers)—and to changes in the vegetation of near-shore areas.

In addition, an increasing demand for protein arose. Traditionally gotten from fishing practiced at a sustainable level, the situation became critical when populations of some of the best food fish species dramatically collapsed. By the 1950s at least one species was commercially extinct. In order to provide people with a regular supply of cheap animal protein, two food fish species were introduced into the lake: *Tilapia* and the Nile perch.

For nearly 30 years there appeared to be no major change in the lake's endemic fauna. However, in 1980 a survey revealed a sudden drop in haplochromine cichlids. From originally forming about 80 percent by weight of catches, they had dropped to 1 percent, with 80 percent represented by the Nile perch.

The Nile perch fishing industry has become hugely important to the local economy. However, a large Nile perch consumes vast quantities of smaller fish. They are therefore blamed for the large-scale decimation leading to the extinction of about 50 percent of the lake's haplochromines. As a result, the Nile perch has turned to other foods, including its own young.

Ray of Hope

For the cichlids the future is still uncertain. Several national and international projects are, however, addressing factors concerning their continued survival. One such development is a wide-ranging captive-breeding program. Some 40 species have already been bred; and while rates of success vary, this is encouraging news. Additionally, aquaculture is being encouraged among the fishermen of the lake in the hope of reducing pressure on remaining cichlid stocks.

The Lake Victoria situation is complex. Yet with appropriate encouragement and dedication further losses may be prevented in the years to come.

Clam, Giant

Tridacna gigas

The strange, massive, and beautiful giant clam has fueled the imaginations of storywriters, though its reputation for closing its giant shells around the limbs of unfortunate explorers is unfounded. Easily collected by souvenir hunters, large giant clams are now rare.

The giant clam, which belongs to the phylum Mollusca, is distinctive for its size and bright color. The animals are giants among invertebrates, showing the basic bivalve mollusk body plan, but on a huge scale. Giant clams are found in tropical seas, where they live in shallow water among reef-building corals. Two massive, thick valves (shells) are hinged together to protect the soft body. In living specimens the gape of the shells reveals bright and often vividly colored flesh.

Giant clams are generally sedentary, living attached to rocks and corals with the hinge downward and the free open edges of the valves upward. Smaller individual clams attach to the substratum by a byssus (a mass of strong threads that are secreted by the clam). Using grinding movements of the shell, they burrow slightly so as to nestle into the rocky reef surface. Large specimens are heavy enough not to need attachment.

Slow-Growing Giants

Giant clams are very slow growing: The thick shells are gently secreted as calcium carbonate by the outer skin, or mantle, of the clam. This exposed part of the mantle tissue contains iridescent colors created by colorless crystalline solid purine. The crystals act like minute lenses; they concentrate any perceptible light that penetrates the water on the myriad microscopic plants that live in the mantle tissue in a symbiotic relationship with the clam. The plants, known as zooxanthellae, make sugars and proteins, and ultimately form part of the giant clam's food supply. Eventually, the photosynthetic products (those created

using sunlight as an energy source) find their way into the clam's energy budget. In return the clam supplies them with carbon dioxide for photosynthesis and the nitrogen and minerals they need to make proteins.

Giant clams are filter feeders, and the other element of the clam's food comes from microscopic plankton that are drawn into the body via the inhaling siphon and the gills. The gills are covered with cells bearing beating cilia (fine threadlike extensions) that drive the water across them and serve to sort and select suitable food particles that are then directed to the gastric tract. The gills are also responsible for gas exchange; while collecting food, the clams take up oxygen and release carbon dioxide. The exhaust water stream leaves via the exhaling siphon. Both siphon openings can be seen when the clam shells gape.

Easy Targets

Unlike many other bivalves, the adults are virtually immobile, so they are easy game for souvenir hunters. Their shells have been used in native societies as house decorations and even as baptismal fonts! They have also been exploited since the 1960s to supply the Taiwanese market's demand for giant clam adductor muscle for human consumption. In 1983 the International Union for the Conservation of Nature (IUCN) identified severe depletion of the species, particularly in the coral reefs of Indonesia, the Philippines, Papua New Guinea, Micronesia, and southern Japan. Fortunately, techniques for cultivating the giant clam were developed during the late 1980s. They are now cultivated in hatcheries in the Asia-Pacific region and used to restock depleted reefs.

See also: Luxury Products **1:** 46; Mussel, Freshwater **7:** 6

DATA PANEL

Giant clam

Tridacna gigas

Family: Tridacnidae

World population: Unknown

Distribution: Asia-Pacific regions

Habitat: Attached to rocks and corals in shallow water

Size: Length across: may reach 41 in (104 cm). Weight: up to 500 lb (227 kg)

Form: Typical bivalve shell shape with scalloped shells; colored mantle visible at gape

Diet: Minute drifting planktonic organisms and the products of photosynthesis by zooxanthellae (microscopic plants) that live in the mantle

Breeding: Each is hermaphroditic; a free-swimming planula larva results from external fertilization of eggs. It attaches itself to a new substrate and develops into a new colony, which produces new zooids (independent animal bodies)

Related endangered species: Probably many, including red coral (*Corallium rubrum*), which is exploited in the Mediterranean Sea

Status: IUCN VU; CITES II

The giant clam *has thick shells with corrugated edges. It is an imposing resident of shallow sea margins.*

Cockatoo, Salmon-Crested

Cacatua moluccensis

The beautiful salmon-crested cockatoo has lost much of its prime habitat on its Indonesian island homes as a result of logging. It is a sought-after species for the flourishing cage-bird trade; trapping now poses an even greater threat to its continued survival.

In the wild the salmon-crested cockatoo is found today only on the large, mountainous island of Seram in the eastern part of Indonesia and at a site on Ambon, one of Seram's three offshore islands, where it used to occur. The islands are part of the South Moluccas (Maluku) island group, and the handsome crested bird is often known as the Moluccan or Seram cockatoo.

Until the late 1970s the salmon-crested cockatoo was common over most of its range, feeding and roosting in flocks of up to 16 birds—except in the breeding season. Nowadays, it survives in much smaller numbers and has been driven out of many of its former haunts in the primary rain forest by extensive logging. Although some birds have been recorded in recently logged areas, they occur at a far lower density than in primary habitat.

Popular Cage Bird

The salmon-crested cockatoo also has the misfortune of being one of the most highly sought after of all cage birds. In 1982 more than 6,400 were trapped; they accounted for 15 percent of all birds captured on Seram for the international cage-bird trade. The species was extinct over most of its former range by 1985. In October 1989 its situation was regarded as so serious that the cockatoo was listed by CITES, and all trade in the bird was banned.

Since 1987 the government of Indonesia has banned exports, but the law is often flouted. As many as 50 birds a week can be trapped—in just one area—out of a total wild population that may number as few as 2,000. The trappers sell the cockatoos to dealers, who sell the birds to smugglers. The birds are stuffed into plastic pipes and concealed in suitcases, then sent by air to collectors and unscrupulous pet shops worldwide.

The trappers from local villages risk their lives by climbing 200-foot- (60-m)- high trees to net the cockatoos at their nest entrances or to snare them in fishing lines. For their efforts they receive a maximum of $6 per bird. By the time one of their catches has reached a dealer in the United States or elsewhere, it will be sold for between

DATA PANEL

Salmon-crested cockatoo

Cacatua moluccensis

Family: Psittacidae

World population: Fewer than 10,000 birds

Distribution: The Indonesian islands of Seram and Ambon; until recently also on Saparua and Haruku

Habitat: Forests and open woodland, from sea level to 3,300 ft (1,000 m)

Size: Length: 18–20 in (46–52 cm)

Form: Usually pale salmon pink, sometimes white; large, backward-curving crest with deep-pink central feathers; underwings mostly deep salmon pink; undertail orange pink; female slightly larger than male

Diet: Seeds, fruit, berries, and nuts; green coconuts in plantations

Breeding: Little known to scientists. Nests in tree hollows, often enlarged to 15 ft (4.5 m) with use of powerful bill. In captivity, known to lay 2 eggs at a time; incubates eggs for 4 weeks; chicks have sparse, yellow down and stay in nest for about 4 months

Related endangered species: Philippine cockatoo (*Cacatua haematuropygia*) CR; yellow-crested cockatoo (*C. sulphurea*) CR; white cockatoo (*C. alba*) VU; Tanimbar cockatoo (*C. goffini*) LRnt

Status: IUCN VU; CITES I

Halmahera

Sula Is

Sulawesi

Buru

Seram

INDONESIA

Flores

See also: Exploitation of Live Animals **1:** 49; Ecotourism **1:** 90; Amazon, St. Vincent **2:** 14; Macaw, Hyacinth **6:** 58

The plumage of the salmon-crested cockatoo *is a delicate pink. The bird also has a backward-curving salmon-pink and white crest that it raises during courtship.*

$1,500 and $2,500. That is, if the bird survives the journey: Most die of starvation, dehydration, suffocation, or disease in transit. Even if they do survive, they may be impossible to keep as pets, since wild-caught cockatoos often pluck their plumage bare, bite holes in their skin, or chew through their perches or their owner's furniture.

Prospects for the Future

There is hope for the future: The California-based project Bird Watch, working with BirdLife International, has initiated a program of research, conservation, and education. Already, it has helped two Seram villages build a rain-forest canopy viewing platform enabling tourists to watch birds and other wildlife. The tourists pay $6 each, plus fees to local guides—as much as a logging company was offering for cutting down a single tree. The villagers decided to pull out of the contract with the loggers that would have cleared the cockatoo's habitat. Other initiatives—including a bird-adoption project—are also planned. Such measures will help raise awareness of the plight of the cockatoo.

The salmon-crested cockatoo breeds well in captivity. Encouraging responsible aviculture (the raising and care of birds in captivity) is an important means of reducing the pressure exerted by bird trapping on the wild population. There is a sizable stock for captive breeding, including over 300 birds in zoos worldwide and perhaps as many as 10,000 in private collections.

Cod, Atlantic

Gadus morhua

Whether freshly caught, deep-frozen, smoked, or dried and salted, the Atlantic cod is a familiar food in Europe and North America. Fishing, intensified to new levels with trawlers developed over the last few decades, has severely depleted stocks of the once-abundant fish.

Atlantic cod have occurred in vast numbers over their extensive range, making them accessible to commercial fisheries in many countries. The species is considered a prime food fish, and its liver is the source of cod-liver oil, a substance rich in vitamins A and D that is used widely as a vitamin supplement. However, evidence suggests that the fish are in greater danger than anyone would have thought. It is also possible that the early years of the 21st century will be, in retrospect, the swan song of the traditional British dish of (cod) fish and chips (fries).

Prolific Migrants

Young cod (codlings) congregate in shallow water, which can extend from close to the low tidal zone to a depth of about 66 feet (20 m). As they mature, these juveniles tend to frequent a much wider range of water depths, moving between 66 and 260 feet (20 and 80 m). Cod can, however, be found at much deeper levels than this, however; some reportedly occur at depths of between 1,640 and 1,970 feet (500 and 600 m).

In terms of temperature tolerance the Atlantic cod is just as versatile and adaptable. Although it prefers water that is between 39 and 45°F (4 to 7°C), it can be found at temperatures of 25 to 61°F (-4 to 16°C). Such tolerance is essential for a species that is a bottom-feeder but whose feeding depth varies widely.

Cod congregate in great shoals (groups of fish) and undertake lengthy migrations to reach their spawning grounds. There the males go through an elaborate courtship dance, involving extending their fins and twisting and turning. A large female cod can produce over 9 million eggs, but the chances of any individual egg or larva surviving are small.

The Great Cod Collapse

In the 19th century, when areas of the North Atlantic were first fished, cod were both abundant and, on average, much larger than today. Some cod weighing up to 200 pounds (90 kg) were recorded. Now, after years of intensive fishing, even a cod of 40 pounds (18 kg) is considered large.

DATA PANEL

Atlantic cod (northern cod)

Gadus morhua

Family: Gadidae

World population: Low enough to be endangered or vulnerable. Newfoundland stocks about 1,700 tons (estimated in 1994)

Distribution: North Atlantic

Habitat: Juveniles live just below the lower tidal zone to about 66 ft (20 m); adults found from 66 ft (20 m) down to 260 ft (80 m): may occur at 1,970 ft (600 m)

Size: Length: 30–70 in (80–180 cm). Weight: 80–211 lb (36–96 kg)

Form: Stout but streamlined fish. Well-developed barbel (whisker) on chin, 3 dorsal (back) and 2 anal (belly) fins. Coloration variable: may be olive-brown or greenish on the back, shading into lighter tones toward the belly: belly is whitish. The base color is overlaid with numerous dark spots

Diet: A bottom-feeder with a strong preference for mollusks, crustacea, worms, and smaller fish

Breeding: Spawns February–April/May at about 660 ft (200 m). In some areas, such as the North Sea, spawning may take place at 66–330 ft (20–100 m). Up to 9 million eggs released by a large female. Eggs and larvae are left to fend for themselves

Related endangered species: Haddock (*Melanogrammus aeglefinus*) VU

Status: IUCN VU; not listed by CITES

See also: Life Strategies **1:** 24; Hunting **1:** 42; Tuna, Northern Bluefin **10:** 8

The Atlantic cod *has a long, tapering body with three dorsal (back) fins. It has long been considered a prime food fish.*

Up until the 1950s annual catches (which averaged about 400 million cod) seemed to have no significant effect on population levels. Then came the factory trawlers, with gigantic nets and onboard processing and freezing facilities. During the mid-1950s and 1960s catches rose dramatically. Soon, however, catches began to drop just as quickly. The situation in the Canadian fishing grounds deteriorated to the point were factory trawlers were excluded from fishing the waters. The domestic fleet continued to fish, but catches were lower.

In the late 1970s the new-generation factory trawlers arrived—the so-called draggers. Their nets trapped huge numbers of fish, but they also plowed up the bottom, destabilizing and destroying the habitats on which the cod and numerous other species depended for their survival. Added to this (although the point is hotly debated), heavy predation by fast-expanding seal populations may have contributed further to the decline in stocks that followed. To make matters worse, delays in implementing scientific recommendations led to severe depletion of cod throughout the Canadian fishing grounds. In 1992 a total ban was imposed on cod fishing around Newfoundland, with further restrictions following in other cod-fishing areas. Thousands of people lost their jobs, and the fishing industry was plunged into crisis. Some estimates suggest that the fish will take about 15 years to recover to commercially viable numbers.

In 2001 the European Union ordered an emergency ban on all deep-sea fishing in more than 40,000 square miles (104,000 sq. km) of the North Sea—the area of the Atlantic between Britain and the Northern European mainland—to prevent the collapse of cod stocks there; in 1999 fishermen had only managed to catch 60 percent of their total European Union quota. It remains to be seen whether fishing controls will guarantee the survival of the Atlantic cod.

55

Cod, Trout

Maccullochella macquariensis

The trout cod was once abundant and widespread in the southern part of the Murray-Darling Basin in New South Wales, Australia, as well as in some major rivers of Victoria. Today only two self-sustaining populations are left, one of which became established from stocks introduced in the early 1900s.

As far back as the mid-19th century fishermen knew of the existence of two types of Murray cod. The smaller one—referred to as the blue-nosed cod—was known as a great fighter, struggling to the point of exhaustion whenever it was caught in a net or hook. The larger type was more passive; people also thought that it tasted better.

It was not until 1972 that the true identities of the two cod were finally unraveled. It turned out that the specimen of Murray cod on which the original species description had been based (the holotype) was, in fact, a trout cod and that there were significant differences between it and the larger Murrays. Hence the trout cod, or blue-nosed cod, and the Murray cod now have separate scientific names.

While not spectacularly colored, the trout cod is a beautiful, impressive animal. It is relatively streamlined and solidly muscled, in keeping with its predatory habits. Its finnage is like the marine groupers and other perchlike fish. The dorsal (back) fin, in particular, has a characteristic spiny front section, followed by a soft, rounded back.

Threats to Survival

The trout cod has been and is still being attacked from several quarters. Overfishing has undoubtedly had a significant effect on populations over the years. Since the trout cod and the Murray cod were long believed to be naturally occurring forms of a single species, angling pressure on the Murray cod has had a carry-over effect on the trout cod. In some areas, such as the Australian Capital Territory, overfishing for Murray

DATA PANEL

Trout cod (blue-nosed cod, rock cod)

Maccullochella macquariensis

Family: Percichthyidae

World population: Figures unknown, but only 2 self-sustaining populations remain

Distribution: A section of the Murray River and Seven Creeks in Victoria, Australia; hatchery-raised stocks have been introduced to some locations in the region

Habitat: Juveniles shelter under boulders and other cover in fast-flowing stretches of river; adults prefer deep pools

Size: Length: 16–20 in (40–50 cm); up to 32 in (80 cm). Weight: 3.3–6.6 lb (1.5–3 kg); up to 35 lb (16 kg)

Form: Streamlined, powerful body. Blue-gray to brown on top, paler below; overlaid by dark spots and streaks. Fins dusky with white, yellow, or orange edges. Head has deep, gray-black stripe running from tip of snout, through eye, to edge of operculum (gill cover)

Diet: Insects, tadpoles, crustaceans, and fish

Breeding: Pair bonding is believed to exist. Spawning thought to be annual, usually in spring or summer, when water temperatures are 57–73°F (14–23°C). Adhesive eggs laid on logs or rocks; eggs hatch after 5–10 days, depending on temperature. Newly hatched fry are 0.2–0.4 in (0.5–1 cm); they begin feeding some 10 days later. Fully mature at 3–5 years

Related endangered species: Clarence River cod *(Maccullochella ikei)* EN; Mary River cod *(M. peelii mariensis)* CR; Oxleyan pygmy perch *(Nannoperca oxleyana)* EN

Status: IUCN EN; not listed by CITES

See also: What Is a Species? **1:** 26; Archerfish, Western **2:** 28; Galaxias, Swan **5:** 16

cod is thought to have been one of the main causes leading to its disappearance from the region's waterways.

Habitat alteration has also played its part. In the case of the trout cod, the construction of dams and other obstructions has had less of an effect than it might have, since the fish is a nonmigratory species. However, other forms of alteration may have had a more pronounced effect. Former shaded and forested areas have been exposed to the sun. As a result, water temperatures have risen, sediment has increased, and the water quality has deteriorated.

Potentially more dangerous are the effects of introduced species of "exotic" fish, not because of competition for food, but from the new disease organisms (pathogens) that they bring with them. As yet, there is no conclusive evidence that the trout cod is affected, but there is cause for concern. Some other Australian species have been shown to be susceptible to a virus infection (epizootic haematopoietic necrosis) first detected in introduced perch.

The trout cod *is distinguished by the spiny dorsal fin on its back. Adult trout cods favor deep pools; juveniles can be found sheltering under boulders in faster stretches of water.*

Conservation Measures

No single measure can be considered adequate when it comes to conserving a species like the trout cod. The approach must be multifaceted, ranging from an understanding of the species' biology and ecology to captive breeding for restocking, angling bans, education, and legislation.

All areas are being tackled; hatchery-bred fish are already being used to restock several trout cod habitats. Monitoring will demonstrate over the next few years whether or not released specimens are breeding in the wild. Should it be found that they are, and should the accompanying legislative, ecological, and educational measures be implemented, the future for the trout cod could begin to look a little better.

57

Coelacanth

Latimeria chalumnae

Until the late 1930s it was thought that the coelacanth had been extinct for 70 million years. Closely related to the ancestors of land vertebrates and so-called living fossils, the coelacanths alive today are primitive deep-sea bony fish. The name refers to the fish's hollow fin spines (the Greek koilos means "hollow" and akantha means "spine").

In 1938 a fishing boat was trawling at a depth of about 240 feet (70 m) off the coast of South Africa near Port Elizabeth when the crew spotted an unusual fish in the catch; none of them had ever seen one like it before. On returning to port, they informed Marjorie Courtenay-Latimer, curator of the local natural history museum. She could not identify it.

Marjorie Courtenay-Latimer measured, examined, and photographed the fish and then had it stuffed. She also wrote to James Leonard Brierly Smith, an ichthyologist (fish specialist) in Grahamstown in South Africa, enclosing a sketch.

The fish measured about 5 feet (1.5 m) in length and was mauvish-blue with iridescent silver markings. Its odd-looking fins were perhaps its most unusual feature. The caudal (tail) fin had an extra portion sticking out at the end, like an additional fin lobe. There were also two dorsal (back) fins, instead of one. The paired fins were even more strange in that they had "stems" that looked like limbs, with fin rays fanning out at the edges.

Fossil Record

The rest, as they say, is history. The fish was a coelacanth, a primitive marine bony fish of the genus *Latimeria*. Fish of the genus *Coelacanthus* had been found as fossils in rocks from the end of the Permian period—225 million years ago—and at the end of the Jurassic period 136 million years ago. The coelacanths were believed to have become extinct about 70 million years ago, so the find was a rare creature, a "living fossil." As such, it provoked much public interest. The modern coelacanth was larger than most fossil fish and had a powerful body.

Reports of other catches of coelacanths have been recorded in more recent years. However, none of the catches has occurred in South Africa until the latest finds in Sodurana Bay. Until the late 1990s the 200 or so finds all came from the waters around Comoros, a small group of islands between southeastern Africa and Madagascar in the Indian Ocean. However, in September 1997 Mark

---

DATA PANEL

Coelacanth

Latimeria chalumnae

Family: Latimeriidae

World population: Unknown, but estimated at 200–500

Distribution: Comoro Islands, Indian Ocean (between Madagascar and southeastern Africa)

Habitat: Cold waters in deep ocean at 240 ft (70 m)

Size: Length: up to 5.9 ft (1.8 m). Weight: 210 lb (95 kg)

Form: Primitive fish with limblike pectoral fins. Bluish base color with light pinkish-white patches

Diet: Fish

Breeding: Livebearer (gives birth to living young). Up to 20 large eggs, each measuring 3.5 in (9 cm) in diameter and weighing 10.6–12.4 oz (300–350 g) are released from ovaries into oviduct. Developing embryos reach a length of at least 12 in (30 cm) before birth. Life span at least 11 years

Related endangered species: Sulawesi coelacanth (*Latimeria menadoensis*) not listed by IUCN

Status: IUCN CR; CITES I

TANZANIA

COMOROS

MOZAMBIQUE

MADAGASCAR

See also: Speciation **1:** 26; Research **1:** 84; Lungfish, Australian **6:** 50

Erdman, a scientist visiting the Indonesian island of Sulawesi, saw an unusual-looking fish being taken into the local market; he immediately identified it as a coelacanth. In 1998 a further specimen was found near Sulawesi, questioning the long-held belief that coelacanths inhabited a limited range in the Indian Ocean—Sulawesi is separated from the Comoro Islands by more than 6,000 miles (10,000 km). The Sulawesi coelacanths seem to be identical in every way except coloration—they are brown with golden-colored flecks. Analysis of genetic structures, however, indicated that the fish is, in fact, a separate species.

Keeping the Past Alive

Although it is not possible to gauge how abundant coelacanths are (scientists estimate that only between 200 and 500 remain in the western part of their range), there is no doubt that they are very rare.

In recognition of its rarity CITES has listed the coelacanth under Appendix I, thus making trade in the fish illegal. Another protective measure involves the safe release of any specimens accidentally caught by fishermen. The coelacanth favors cold waters at depths of about 240 feet (70 m). A "deep release kit" (first suggested by Raymond Walner, a visitor to one of the coelacanth websites) allows specimens to be lowered rapidly in a sack to a depth where the water is sufficiently cold and where the fish can release itself safely. So far the method has proved to be the most effective way of returning coelacanths to the wild.

Coelacanths found today have changed little from their ancestors, although they are larger than most "fossil fish." They have powerful bodies and limblike fins, which they use to move themselves around on the sea bottom when they are looking for prey.

Condor, California

Gymnogyps californianus

The California condor has already been extinct in the wild once, and only the reintroduction and management of captive-bred birds is preventing its disappearance for a second time.

There is evidence that the massive California condor once lived across a wide range in the United States. Since 1937, however, it has been confined to California in the nation's southwestern corner. This decline in range was matched throughout the 20th century by a continuing fall in numbers, driven by human activity and in particular by the widespread availability of firearms. Many birds were shot and killed; others suffered indirectly by ingesting lead from the carcasses of animals that had been shot and abandoned, leading to death by lead poisoning. By 1987 the California condor's situation had become so critical that the last six wild individuals were captured for inclusion in a captive-breeding program. The magnificent creature had formally become extinct in the wild.

At that time there were already 16 birds in captivity, so the total population stood at only 22 birds. Since then a large-scale, integrated breeding and reintroduction program has been in operation. It has had notable success; the total population has increased almost sevenfold to 147 birds. Of them 97 are still in captivity, split between three breeding facilities managed respectively by the Peregrine Fund at the World Center for Birds of Prey, by the Los Angeles Zoo, and by the San Diego Wild Animal Park. The remaining 50 birds have been reintroduced back to the wild at five separate sites. There are now 28 birds in California, at Lion Canyon, in Los Padres Natural Forest, and at Castle Crags on the western border of San Luis Obispo County. The other 22 are in northern Arizona, at Vermillion Cliffs and at Hurricane Cliffs 60 miles (100 km) to the west.

Problems in the Wild

Unfortunately, the recovery program is all that is stopping the species from becoming extinct in the wild for a second time, since the released birds still depend on the ongoing work of the program for their continued survival. None of the birds has yet reached reproductive maturity, and in addition they all currently rely on food provided by the program. Nor have they found it easy to readapt

---

DATA PANEL

California condor

Gymnogyps californianus

Family: Cathartidae

World population: At the end of 1998 the total population was 147, including 50 in the wild

Distribution: Birds have been reintroduced in 5 areas, 3 in California and 2 in northern Arizona

Habitat: Rocky, open-country scrubland terrain, coniferous forests, and oak savanna

Size: Length: 46–54 in (117–134 cm); wingspan: 9 ft (2.7 m). Weight: 17.6–31 lb (8–14 kg)

Form: Huge, unmistakable raptor (bird of prey). Mostly black with white wing-linings and silvery panel on upper secondaries. The head is naked and orange-red. Immatures have black heads and dark mottling on the underwing. When soaring, the wings are held horizontally, with the outermost wing feathers curled up

Diet: Scavenges the carcasses of large mammals, although the reintroduced birds currently rely on food provided by the recovery program

Breeding: Nest sites are located in cavities in cliffs, on rocky outcrops, or in large trees. Clearly adapted for very low reproductive output

Related endangered species: Andean condor (*Vultur gryphus*) LRnt

Status: IUCN CR; CITES I and II

to conditions in the wild. The first birds to be released suffered from behavioral difficulties and tended to collide with powerlines. This had not previously been a problem with the species and such accidents may have been caused by the captive-bred birds getting used to man-made structures. Following the deaths of a number of newly released individuals, a program of "aversion training" was introduced that has involved conditioning the birds to avoid powerlines and all contact with humans. The first of the conditioned birds was released in 1995, and so far the training appears to have been successful.

Other grounds for optimism include the fact that at some of the release sites the birds are increasingly finding food of their own. In addition, at certain times of the year they are now ranging up to 250 miles (400 km) away from the sites. In the meantime the provision of clean carcasses does have the added benefit of avoiding any possibility of lead poisoning.

Ambitious Targets

The current conservation action plan for the species has set several ambitious targets. A long-term goal is to establish two self-sustaining populations of at least 150 individuals each, including 15 breeding pairs. For this goal to be realized, all aspects of

California condors

came close to extinction in the late 1980s, when the total population of the species was reduced to just 22 birds.

the current program must be continued. One key factor is the maintenance of the birds' habitat. Another is the implementation of information and education programs, which will raise awareness of the California condor's plight. Without such efforts persecution may begin again as the birds become increasingly widespread.

Coot, Horned

Fulica cornuta

The horned coot is restricted to a few freshwater and brackish (slightly salty) lakes in the high Andes of South America, where populations fluctuate between periods of drought and flooding.

The horned coot is the world's second largest species of the genus of stocky, black-plumaged aquatic birds within the family Raillidae that are known as coots. Along with its larger cousin—the aptly named giant coot—it is a high-mountain specialist, found on the borders of Argentina, Bolivia, and Chile. It occurs mainly in the cold, desert plateau region known as the puna at altitudes of 9,800 to 17,000 feet (3,000 to 5,200 m). In winter, when lakes freeze and the birds can no longer obtain food, they sometimes move as low as 6,500 feet (2,000 m).

Within its restricted habitat the horned coot is further limited because it lives only on freshwater and brackish lakes, while most of the lakes in the region are highly salty. The bird depends on a staple diet of submerged aquatic plants that cannot tolerate salt water, which is probably why it avoids the saltier lakes.

By day horned coots are reluctant to take to the air. Instead, they move around the lake by skimming along the surface, propelling themselves by their powerful legs. At night, however, they may fly considerable distances from one lake to another in search of food: Flocks of the birds have been seen arriving at a new lake at dusk, staying overnight and the next day, and leaving the following night.

An unusual feature of the horned coot, from which it gets both its common and specific names, is the long black "horn" or proboscis that extends from the base of its bill, where it joins two black, fleshy wattles (loose folds of skin). All three protuberances end in tufts of thick black bristles. The proboscis usually rests along the ridge of the upper mandible (jaw) of the bill, but can be erected and

DATA PANEL

Horned coot

Fulica cornuta

Family: Rallidae

World population: About 10,000 birds

Distribution: Andes of southwestern Bolivia, north Chile, and northwestern Argentina

Habitat: High-altitude freshwater or brackish lakes

Size: Length: 18–21 in (46–53 cm). Weight: 3.5–4.6 lb (1.6–2.1 kg)

Form: Large, heavy-bodied, small-headed coot with slate-gray plumage; darker on head and neck apart from undertail coverts (smaller feathers around base of larger feathers), which are black with 2 white stripes; bill greenish yellow with dull-orange base, black ridge, and long, extensible proboscis that has 2 black tufts at base; sturdy legs and feet. Juveniles

grayer with large area of white on chin and throat; greenish-black bill; proboscis smaller or absent

Diet: Poorly known; aquatic plants, especially pondweeds, water milfoils, and *Ruppia* (a type of grass); some aquatic grasses and seeds

Breeding: Breeds mainly October–February in colonies of up to 90 pairs; both sexes build vast, cone-shaped mound of stones ending just beneath the water's surface, on top of which they construct a huge nest of submerged water plants. Female lays 3–5 eggs that are gray to buff, speckled with dark gray-brown; incubation period unknown; chicks fed by both parents

Related endangered species: Hawaiian coot (*Fulica alae*) VU; Caribbean coot (*F. caribaea*) LRnt; Mascarene coot (*F. newtoni*) EX

Status: IUCN LRnt; not listed by CITES

See also: Populations **1:** 20; Boom and Bust **1:** 21; Corncrake **3:** 66; Rail, Guam **8:** 18; Takahe **9:** 48

extended. Its function is uncertain, although there are records of the bird using it to help carry vegetation when nest building, and it may be raised during courtship or other displays.

Huge Nest

More remarkable still is the horned coot's nest, one of the most extraordinary of any bird. A pair collects huge numbers of stones from the lake shore or bed to form an underwater platform. Picking them up one by one, the birds transport the stones to the nest site and position them to form a massive conical structure, measuring up to 13 feet (4 m) across at its base and about 2 feet (0.6 m) high. The whole structure may contain up to 1.7 tons (1,730 kg) of stones.

The nest itself takes the shape of a truncated cone. Measuring about 6.5 feet (2 m) at the base and 1 to 2 feet (30 to 60 cm) high, it is built of clumps of waterweed, which the pair collect with their bills. Throughout the breeding season the pair will add fresh weed to the nest, tearing off the seed pods to feed to their young. The extraordinary structures are often used for years on end and, when empty, serve as nest sites for other waterbirds.

Vulnerable to Change

The total number of horned coots is unknown, but the birds generally breed in small colonies; some sites hold only one to 10 nesting pairs, while few contain as many as 70 or 80 pairs. Until relatively recently it was thought that there may be fewer than 5,000 individuals in the world. Occasionally, however, large concentrations have been recorded, especially the 2,800 birds on Laguna Pelada, Bolivia, in 1989 and the 8,988 birds and 180 active nests at a remote lake in the Vilama and Pululos area of Argentina in 1995.

Firm evidence of an overall decline is lacking, but local populations are thought to fluctuate widely between periods of drought and flooding. In addition to natural hazards, the birds are subjected to a number of human-induced threats, including hunting, egg harvesting, water abstraction, and the trampling of lakeside vegetation by cattle. A few breeding lakes get some protection, but more needs to be done to ensure that the species is not pushed into decline.

The horned coot *is so called because of an unusual hornlike appendage on its bill. A pair build a massive, conical nest of waterweed on top of a huge mound of stones.*

Cormorant, Galápagos

Phalacrocorax harrisi

Isolated for thousands of years by the remoteness of its native islands, the Galápagos cormorant lacks both an instinct for danger and an ability to fly. Its refuge has now been invaded by people, pollution, and alien predators, and its naturally small population has fluctuated dramatically in recent years.

The Galápagos Islands are renowned for their unique wildlife, yet few of their native species are more spectacularly odd than the flightless Galápagos cormorant. It lives only on Fernandina and the north and west shores of Isabela, on the western side of the equatorial Galápagos. The shores are bathed by the cool, nutrient-rich waters of both the Cromwell and Humboldt Currents. The nutrients support a lush growth of plankton that feeds vast shoals of small fish, so for much of the year the seas around the cormorant colonies are teeming with food.

For the Galápagos cormorant the land is just somewhere to breed; it feeds in inshore waters. Like all cormorants, it hunts underwater for fish, diving beneath the surface and driving itself along with its webbed feet. Wings just get in the way while fishing, so over the millennia those of the Galápagos cormorant have been reduced to threadbare stumps. Its wing muscles have dwindled too, along with the deep keelbone to which they were attached. All the energy has been diverted into its legs and feet, which are unusually big and strong. They give the cormorant the power to swim right down to the rocky seabed, flush a fish or octopus from a crevice, and pursue and catch it in its hooked bill before surfacing to eat it.

Climatic Hazard

Galápagos cormorants typically breed between the months of March and September, when the cool, rich ocean currents guarantee their food supply. However, in December the trade winds that drive the Humboldt Current retreat southward, allowing warmer, virtually sterile surface water to flow in from the north. This seasonal current is called El Niño. It usually lasts for just four to six weeks, but every four or five years an exceptionally powerful El Niño event disrupts the marine ecosystem for up to nine months. The plankton supply fails, the fish vanish, and the seabirds starve.

The cormorants have had to cope with regular setbacks since they arrived on the islands, and

DATA PANEL

Galápagos cormorant

Phalacrocorax harrisi

Family: Phalacrocoracidae

World population: Under 1,000 birds

Distribution: Coastlines of Fernandina and Isabela in the Galápagos Islands

Habitat: Breeds on ledges of volcanic rock just above shoreline; feeds in inshore waters

Size: Length: 35–39 in (89–100 cm); each wing averages 10 in (25 cm) in length. Weight: 5.5–8.8 lb (2.5–4 kg)

Form: Heaviest of all cormorants (males heavier than females). Powerful hooked bill and long, thick, sinuous neck; long, broad tail; strong, fully webbed feet; reduced weak wings with sparse plumage; blackish brown plumage with bare throat patch; pale green-blue eyes. Juveniles glossy black with brown eyes

Diet: Marine fish, mainly bottom-dwelling species such as eels and rockfish; also octopus and squid

Breeding: March–September. Nests in groups of up to 12 pairs, building bulky nests of seaweed on remote sites near shore. Up to 4, usually 2–3 whitish eggs incubated for 5 weeks by both sexes; young fledge at 8.5 weeks, but stay at nest for a further 4.5 weeks, where they are often fed by male alone

Related endangered species: Nine, including bank cormorant (*Phalacrocorax neglectus*) VU; Socotra cormorant (*P. nigrogularis*) VU

Status: IUCN EN; not listed by CITES

COSTA RICA
PANAMA
COLOMBIA
Galápagos Islands (Ecuador)
ECUADOR
PERU

See also: Island Biogeography **1:** 30; Pollution **1:** 50; Introductions **1:** 54; Pelican, Dalmatian **7:** 62

they show an amazing ability to recover. In 1982 a catastrophic El Niño event slashed their population from some 850 to a perilously low total of 400 adults, but 18 months later the population had more than doubled to about 1,000 birds. There was another unusually extreme El Niño event in 1997, and some researchers fear that global climate change may be increasing the frequency of such events.

Enemy Aliens

Even at their peak, Galápagos cormorants have never been numerous. They are also restricted to just 230 miles (370 km) of coastline on their native islands. This makes them vulnerable to any local disaster such as the oil spill caused by the grounding of the oil tanker *Jessica* on San Cristobal Island in January 2001. San Cristobal is on the eastern side of the Galapágos, but the winds and currents drove the oil slicks west, threatening the southern and eastern shores of Isabela. The cormorants had a narrow escape, since they inhabit the northern and western shores.

Oil is not their only problem. Diving cormorants regularly drown in stray fishing nets and lobster traps. Commercial fishing is illegal, but the waters are so rich in tuna and other valuable species that they attract operators prepared to flout the rules.

Fishermen may also import alien predators such as rats, cats, and even wild dogs. Lacking both the instinct to escape danger and the ability to fly, the cormorants, their eggs, and their young are vulnerable to such threats.

Another problem is tourism. Although it helps fund the conservation of the Galápagos, tourism causes disturbance and also adds to the pollution problem; much of the oil spilled by the *Jessica* was a delivery of fuel for tourist vessels.

The Galápagos cormorant *has little use for its wings, the muscles of which are weak. When fishing, the bird employs its strong legs and feet.*

Corncrake

Crex crex

Corncrakes are considerably more numerous than was thought a few years ago, but changes in agricultural practices are likely to trigger rapid population declines in the near future.

The corncrake occupies one of the largest ranges of any threatened species. It breeds from Ireland, Britain, France, and possibly Spain in western Europe east to Asiatic Russia, Mongolia, and China. The species migrates south in the nonbreeding season to the southern parts of sub-Saharan Africa, and birds have been recorded on passage in a large number of countries throughout northern Africa and the Middle East.

The birds' numbers are exceptionally large for a threatened species. The total European population is estimated to be between 1.1 and 1.8 million singing males, with a further 0.5 to 1.2 million in Asia. Since corncrakes are generally elusive, the only effective method of surveying them is by listening for the far-carrying calls of the male. However, conservationists have not always known that the population was so

large. As recently as 1996 the best estimate was 92,000 to 233,000 singing males. The discrepancy in numbers raises two questions: Why have the estimates increased so dramatically in recent years, and why is such a widespread and numerous species still considered threatened?

The first question is the easiest to answer. The recent upward revision of numbers results from improved surveying of the species and increased collaboration among conservationists. In 1996 the European Union and the Council of Europe endorsed an action plan that has led to a host of national action plans across the continent. In 1998 a Corncrake Conservation Team was established, bringing together researchers, ornithologists, and conservation organizations working across the species' great range. In addition, the species is covered by what is probably

DATA PANEL

Corncrake

Crex crex

Family: Rallidae

World population: Estimated at 3.2–6 million birds, with numbers in Asia especially uncertain

Distribution: Breeds over a huge range in Europe and Asia; winters in sub-Saharan Africa

Habitat: Agricultural grassland managed for hay production in Europe; some wetlands and other grasslands and savannas in Africa

Size: Length: 10.5–12 in (27–30 cm); wingspan: 16.5–21 in (42–53 cm). Weight: male 4.5–7.5 oz (130–210 g); female 5–5.5 oz (138–158 g)

Form: Upperparts brown with black streaking; underparts pale brown with cinnamon barring on flanks; some gray and reddish facial markings. The

reddish wings, combined with dangling legs in flight, are distinguishing features of the species. More likely to be heard than seen; its repetitive, far-carrying, "crex-crex" cry is given mainly at night and in the early morning

Diet: In the breeding season a wide range of invertebrates; mostly seeds in the fall and winter

Breeding: Believed to be polygamous (has more than 1 mate), with some males moving far to new singing areas. Nest is built on ground in dense vegetation from dead stems and leaves. Average clutch size 10 eggs; possibly 2 broods per season

Related endangered species: Forty-five in the family Rallidae, including snoring rail (*Aramidopsis palteni*) VU; austral rail (*Rallus antarcticus*) VU; and Inaccessible rail (*Atlantisia rogersi*) VU

Status: IUCN VU; not listed by CITES

See also: Communities and Ecosystems **1:** 22; Coot, Horned **3:** 62; Takahe **9:** 48

the most powerful international piece of legislation currently affecting threatened birds: the European Union's Wild Birds Directive. The combined efforts of people in many countries have resulted in improved reporting and conservation.

The Threat from Intensive Agriculture

The other question as to why the species is still considered threatened is altogether more complex. First, there is evidence of long-term decline in Europe. Between 1970 and the early 1990s 22 European countries, including those with the largest populations, such as Russia and Belarus, saw declines of between 20 and 50 percent. The falls were caused mainly by the intensification of agriculture, since throughout Europe the species primarily depends on grassland managed for hay production. The mechanization of hay and silage mowing and the practice of starting mowing earlier in the year are both significant threats, reducing nesting success and the survival rates of chicks and adults.

There are also concerns that such practices are extending to other parts of the corncrake's range. As land that was abandoned following privatization in eastern Europe and Russia becomes overgrown or is returned to intense management, numbers are likely to fall rapidly. Overgrown habitats will become too scrublike, while, as trends in western Europe have shown, the species is unable to adapt to intensive agricultural areas.

Improved habitat-management techniques have been investigated in response to the corncrake's threatened status; it is known, for example, that mowing fields from the center outward reduces the killing of chicks. The development and introduction of such strategies are the key to maintaining healthy corncrake populations in the future.

Across much of Eurasia *the corncrake is known for its repetitive rasping "crex-crex" cry, uttered by male birds in the springtime breeding season for hours on end.*

Courser, Jerdon's

Rhinoptilus bitorquatus

The enigmatic Jerdon's courser made ornithological history when it was recently rediscovered in eastern India after being thought extinct since the early 20th century. However, it may yet be lost as a result of habitat destruction and disturbance.

The rediscovery of the rare Jerdon's courser was one of the most exciting ornithological events of recent years. The delicately built wader, with its distinctive double breast-band, was first discovered for science in about 1848 by Thomas Jerdon, a Scottish army surgeon who was one of the major pioneers of Indian ornithology.

In the 50 years following his discovery Jerdon's courser was seen and collected intermittently within a restricted area to the north of Madras in the states of Andhra Pradesh and Maharashtra, mainly between the Godavari and Penner River systems in the low mountain system of the Eastern Ghats. A bird observed in the Penner River Valley in 1900 by an English ornithologist, Howard Campbell, represented the last known record of the species, and from then on Jerdon's courser was assumed to be extinct.

Inspired by the Indian ornithologist Dr. Salim Ali, the Bombay Natural History Society decided to carry out investigations to discover more about the status of Jerdon's courser. Searches took place during the 1980s in the areas where the courser had previously been recorded. Although preliminary surveys could find no trace of the species, when illustrated posters were distributed to local people, a number of them claimed to have seen the bird. On the strength of their evidence field surveys were done, and in the early hours of January 13, 1986, near the Lankamalai Hills a single Jerdon's courser was spotted in the beam of a flashlight and captured.

Subsequent searches have usually been conducted in the hours of darkness, since the species appears to feed at night—a habit that could help explain its elusiveness. Sightings of birds at six further localities in three hill ranges of southern Andhra Pradesh revealed what is probably a single, small population.

INDIA

SRI LANKA

DATA PANEL

Jerdon's courser

Rhinoptilus bitorquatus

Family: Glareolidae

World population: Estimated at 50–250

Distribution: Eastern Ghats (mountain range) of states of Andhra Pradesh and extreme southern Madhya Pradesh in eastern India

Habitat: Rolling, rocky foothills with dense scrub forest and bushes (including thorny and nonthorny species), interspersed with open areas of bare ground

Size: Length: about 10.5 in (27 cm)

Form: Slender-bodied, smallish, ploverlike bird; shortish, yellow-based, black arched bill; longish, pale-yellowish legs. Plumage has complex pattern with distinctive pair of brown breast bands (the upper one much broader) separated by a white band; mainly blackish-brown crown and hind neck; broad, white eyestripes and broad, blackish-brown band behind each eye; orange-chestnut patch on white throat; upperparts mainly brown, apart from pattern of breast banding, underparts

mainly white; in flight, brown wings with black primary flight feathers that have white patch near tips; black tail with white base

Diet: Poorly known; feeds at night, probably on insects

Breeding: Unconfirmed report of clutch of 2 eggs said to have been collected in 1895

Related endangered species: Not a courser, but in same family: black-winged pratincole *(Glareola nordmanni)* DD

Status: IUCN CR; not listed by CITES

See also: Research **1:** 84; Saving the Habitats **1:** 88; Murrelet, Japanese **7:** 4; Plover, Piping **7:** 84

Habitat Destruction

It is likely that Jerdon's courser was never numerous. Its small, localized populations were possibly driven to the verge of extinction by overgrazing and disturbance in the special habitat it favors. The bird prefers scrubby forest (including dense thorn bushes, especially of *Carissa*, *Zizyphus*, and *Acacia*) for sheltering from danger and patches of bare, open ground where it can find insect prey.

Today the courser's habitat is under greater threat than ever, being increasingly scarce and fragmented. After a dam was built in the region at Somasilla, the inhabitants of 57 villages were relocated to areas within the bird's range. The settlers depend on the surrounding landscape for fuel and grazing land for their livestock; such uses are likely to put increasing pressure on the remaining courser population. A further threat to the habitat comes from extensive quarrying operations. In addition, the increased disturbance by the villagers may directly affect the birds themselves.

Urgent Measures

In an effort to pull the little-known bird back from the brink of extinction, a wildlife sanctuary and national park were established in the region in response to the species' rediscovery. Concerted lobbying of the authorities by conservation groups has ensured that plans for a canal to pass through one of the protected areas were revised and that the canal was realigned. Already members of the local community have been employed to try and find more of the coursers.

Surveys to discover the bird's precise distribution, population size, and ecological needs in its presumed range are urgent if Jerdon's courser is to survive. An assessment of the different threats it faces is also crucial. As well as working to prevent the expansion of quarrying and mining operations, there is a need to protect areas where the birds are found. One measure is to persuade local communities to reduce habitat destruction and disturbance.

Jerdon's courser *was thought to be extinct. More needs to be known about the bird to help protect it, including its distribution and breeding habits.*

Cow, Steller's Sea

Hydrodamalis gigas

The sea cow was a close relative of today's manatees and dugongs, and it lived in the North Pacific. It was discovered in 1741 and was extinct less than 30 years later.

In 1741 an expedition led by the Danish explorer Vitus Bering was shipwrecked on the Commander Islands off Siberia in the Bering Sea. Bering and his crew were stranded on a bleak and inhospitable coast for the whole of the following winter until they were able to rebuild their boat and escape.

The expedition's doctor and scientist was a young German naturalist called Georg Steller. He was the only naturalist ever to see sea cows alive. He had plenty of time to observe them, since the expedition depended on killing sea cows to provide food for its survival. Assuming that there were sea cows all around the islands, there may have been as many as 2,000 of them at this time. However, this represented the dying remnants of what had once been a much more widespread species. The sea cows had been eliminated from most areas, including Japanese waters, and by Steller's time it seems that they were already restricted to the Commander Islands.

The sea cow is the only type of sirenian (marine mammals that are not seals or whales, including today's manatees and dugongs) that lived in cold water. They were large, cumbersome creatures that could not come ashore like seals. Instead, they drifted slowly around in the sheltered bays along the rocky coast, moving through the offshore kelp beds, munching almost continuously on the long strands of seaweed. Steller's sea cows had no teeth, just big, horny plates with large ridges and troughs in each jaw that were used to crush the seaweeds on which they fed. In winter they became emaciated as the kelp beds died back.

Seaweed is not very nutritious, so the animals had to take in vast quantities each day to get the nutrients they needed. They spent almost all their time feeding with their head underwater, surfacing only occasionally to breathe with a loud snort. The animal's back, up to 10 feet (3 m) long, arched out of the water like a huge floating log.

It was possible for the sailors to row a boat among the herds without risk of being attacked. The sea cows were slow moving and completely harmless and had no fear of people. They allowed the sailors to

RUSSIA

Kamchatka Peninsula

Commander Islands last known range

Aleutian Islands (U.S.)

DATA PANEL

Steller's sea cow
Hydrodamalis gigas

Family: Dugongidae

World population: 0 (Extinct)

Distribution: Formerly along the coast of the Commander (Komandorskiye) and Aleutian Islands in the Bering Sea, North Pacific Ocean. Fossil evidence from California

Habitat: Rocky coasts with extensive seaweed beds

Size: Total length of a female, probably the only one ever measured: 24.6 ft (7.5 m); circumference of body: 20.3 ft (6. 2 m); Probably grew larger sometimes. Weight: probably up to 11 tons (10 tonnes)

Form: A large, whalelike animal with small, blunt head and forked tail flipper. Forelimbs formed paddles; no hind limbs. Skin thick and brown, sometimes blotchy. Sparse, bristly hairs

Diet: Various seaweeds

Breeding: Probably only 1 young at long intervals. Life span unknown, but likely to have been at least 20 years

Related endangered species: Dugong *(Dugong dugon)** VU; Amazon manatee *(Trichechus inunguis)* VU; American manatees *(T. manatus*—includes Florida manatee *T. manatus latirostris)** VU; African manatee *(T. senegalensis)* VU

Status: IUCN EX; not listed by CITES

See also: Specialization 1: 28; Hunting 1: 42; Dugong 4: 46; Manatee, Florida 6: 68

Steller's sea cows *were the largest of the sirenians. They moved slowly through the shallow, cold water, and browsed seaweeds, a peculiar form of feeding that is not shared by any other large animals.*

approach close enough to snare them one at a time with an iron hook on a long rope. The stricken sea cow was then speared.

Steller tells us that the animals lived in small family groups, with adult males and females accompanied by young. He thought that they had only one baby at a time and probably took at least a year to raise it. Such slow reproduction was probably adequate, bearing in mind that there would have been few natural predators in these waters that could tackle such a large, thick-skinned animal. However, such a low rate of reproduction and slow growth would have been insufficient to compensate for losses of the animals when the humans began more intensive hunting.

There for the Taking

The crew of the Bering expedition had also seen fur seals in the northern waters. When they reached the mainland, news of the fur seals spread, and expeditions set out to catch these valuable creatures. They too found sea cows an easy target and a good source of food. The animals' thick skins, almost like tree bark, made useful shoe leather and boat covers. Sea cows had to surface to breathe air, so hunters in boats could reach and spear them easily. The sea cows were said to help each other when one was distressed, so it was easy to kill several at a time. The remaining population had been wiped out by 1768.

Lost Creatures

The treacherous and inhospitable shores of the North Pacific are rarely explored, even today. The weather is poor all year round, with almost constant drizzle and fog. It is possible that sea cows survived longer in some remote bays, and sailors reported sightings even into the 20th century. However, it is virtually certain that the sea cow no longer exists.

71

Crab, California Bay Pea

Parapinnixa affinis

Pea crabs are tiny crabs, almost always less than half an inch (1 cm) wide. As adults they live associated with other marine animals such as bivalve mollusks (clams) and tubeworms.

The California Bay pea crab inhabits the tubes and burrows of polychaete worms (marine annelid worms of the class Polychaeta that bear bristles and have paired appendages). Other species of pea crab, such as *Pinnotheres pisum*, are found in mussel and cockle shells in European coastal waters, while females of *Pinnotheres ostreum*, also known as the oyster crab, are found in oysters of the Atlantic coastal waters of North America and are abundant in oysters of Chesapeake Bay. (The males are usually free-swimming.)

Pea crabs live in other animal hosts but do not derive nourishment from their hosts' tissues; animals with this arrangement are not parasites but are known as commensal indwellers. The pea crabs appear to do no serious physical harm or damage to their hosts, although they do not seem to do any particular good either.

Unlike other crabs, which are protected by a hard exoskeleton made from calcium carbonate, pea crabs have a soft body. They rely on their hosts to provide them with shelter and protection.

The pea crabs intercept some of the food sieved from the water by the gills of the host animal. They feed on small prey items such as planktonic animals and carrion scraps that find their way near to or into the host's tube or shell.

Pea crabs sometimes live in pairs, although the male may move around between hosts. The female will carry the fertilized eggs under her abdomen until they hatch. At this point a planktonic larva swims away from the tube or burrow and goes through several stages, feeding on other planktonic organisms until it is sufficiently developed to settle on the seabed and seek out a new invertebrate host.

A study of the morphology (form and structure) of animals can tell us a lot about their lifestyles and adaptations to their favorite habitats. The strange shape of the California Bay pea crab, being much wider than it is long, is a perfect adaptation to life in a tube; It can move up and down its home by walking sideways, particularly aided by the well-developed next

CANADA

UNITED STATES

MEXICO

DATA PANEL

California Bay pea crab

Parapinnixa affinis

Family: Pinnotheridae

World population: Unknown

Distribution: Western seaboard of U.S., especially coast of California

Habitat: The tubes and burrows of marine polychaete worms, including *Terebella californica* and *Amphitrite* species

Size: Minute crabs, reaching about 0.1 in (2.5 mm) long and 0.2 in (5 mm) wide

Form: Minute, wide crabs with very well-developed 4th pair of walking legs quite out of proportion to the rest of their body

Diet: Small marine animals and carrion

Breeding: Male fertilizes eggs that are carried on female's abdomen. Here they are guarded, oxygenated, and protected until they hatch into free-swimming planktonic larvae. They

pass through several stages, feeding on plankton before they metamorphose, settle on the seabed, and seek out a new suitable host worm

Related endangered species: None

Status: IUCN EN; not listed by CITES

See also: Communities and Ecosystems **1:** 22; Specialization **1:** 28; Crayfish, Noble **3:** 78

The California Bay pea crab *(left) is less than 0.20 in (5 mm) wide— about a quarter of the size of the tiny California fiddler crab (below), which is distinguished by its large claw (in the male), used to signal to mates. The fiddler crab lives in burrows in sandy mud in bays and estuaries from Southern California to Baja California. Its future is also uncertain as a result of encroachment on its habitat by human construction.*

to last pair of walking legs. Pea crabs of the species *Pinnotheres pisum* have much more rounded bodies, reflecting the fact that they do not live in such confined spaces.

The relative softness of the California Bay pea crab's shell contributes to its overall flexibility and helps when it moves around in confined spaces. In some pea crab species there is a marked difference in the shape of the claws in the males and females, which probably assists the male in holding the female during mating.

Vulnerability

The viability of pea crabs depends on the availability of hosts as well as the presence of other essentials such as food and reproductive mates. Many of the worm species that the California Bay pea crab relies on are subjected to population fluctuations. These events in turn affect the population of the pea crabs that live with them.

Records of animals as small as pea crabs are often lacking, so it is difficult to establish a broad view of their distribution and abundance. The California Bay pea crab is listed as Endangered by the IUCN, and the extent of threats to the animal will be resolved only as a result of more scientific research.

Crab, Horseshoe

Limulus polyphemus

Despite their name, horseshoe crabs are not crustaceans like other crabs, lobsters, and shrimps. They are related to scorpions, spiders, and the extinct trilobites.

Horseshoe crabs, or king crabs, are among the strangest-looking marine invertebrates. They belong to a class of their own called Merostomata. Different species occur in two distinct parts of the world: the eastern seaboard of North America and in Southeast Asia, which suggests that they are the last surviving representatives of an ancient group that was once widely distributed in the world's oceans. Fossil horseshoe crabs have been found in rocks in Germany dating back to Jurassic times, and the crabs are sometimes referred to as living fossils.

The dominant feature of the crabs is a domed carapace (hard shield), which carries a pair of compound eyes (made up of many separate visual units) at its side and a smaller pair of simple eyes nearer the midline. Behind the domed carapace is a triangular abdomen that bears a pointed tail spine, or telson.

Turning the carapace over reveals that its leading edge is clearly horseshoe shaped; hence the name. There are six pairs of jointed legs, an arrangement that suggests the crab's affinity with spiders and scorpions. The first legs include a pair of small feeding appendages ending in nippers (corresponding to the chelicerae, or fang-bearing appendages of a spider's head); there are five more pairs of appendages, the first of which corresponds to the pedipalps, or leglike sensory limbs of the spider's head. The last pair of appendages bears additional spines to help the crab get a grip on the sand. Just above the "knee joint" there are swollen, toughened extensions called gnathobases that can press together and are used for crushing prey and preparing it for swallowing. Such tools are essential because much of the crab's prey—such as clams and snails—has shells. Under the abdomen are a series of flaplike structures that assist with swimming and fast movement over the sand. They pump water over the respiratory surface of the gill "books"—thin plates well supplied with blood vessels and arranged a bit like the pages in a book. The tail spine stabilizes the crab as it moves around on the sand.

As in many marine animals, reproduction in the horseshoe crab is controlled by

DATA PANEL

Horseshoe crab (king crab)

Limulus polyphemus

Family: Limulidae

World population: Unknown

Distribution: Coastal waters of India, Indonesia, Malaysia, Philippines, Singapore, Thailand, Taiwan, and Vietnam; Atlantic coasts of Canada, U.S., and Mexico

Habitat: Sandy or muddy shores and shallow water in bays and estuaries

Size: Length: up to 60 cm. Weight: adults 0.7–1 oz (20–30 g)

Form: Fossillike, armored invertebrate with conspicuous tail. Six pairs of jointed appendages, including pair of feeding appendages ending in nippers

Diet: Small bivalves, worms, and other invertebrates; occasionally seaweed

Breeding: Males clasp tail of female and are towed around by her. Female digs shallow pit on midshore and lays 200–300 eggs; male sheds sperm over them. Larvae, known as trilobite larvae because they resemble the fossil trilobites, emerge. Several larval stages are marked by molts. Maturity is reached after 16 molts and at about 10 years

Related endangered species: Three other marine invertebrates that share the common name horseshoe crab: *Carcinoscorpius rotundicoruda* DD, *Tachypleus gigas* DD, and *T. tridentatus* DD

Status: IUCN LRnt; not listed by CITES

See also: The Animal Kingdom **1:** 58; Spider, Kauai Cave Wolf **9:** 24

the moon and tides. Breeding takes place in spring and summer. At full moon, when the highest tides occur, females move up the beach to lay their eggs. A male clings onto each female and is dragged up the beach. The female digs a shallow pit just above the high-tide mark and lays her eggs in it. The male fertilizes the eggs as they are laid. Then they are covered with sand and left alone.

Cause for Concern

The future of the horseshoe crab is a cause for concern among conservationists. For many years the animals were regarded as a common sight on the shore and in the shallow water of their native seas.

Horseshoe crabs *congregate at the edge of the tide. They can swim on their backs using their gill flaps, but they also plow through sand or mud, arching their bodies and pushing with the tail spine and last pair of legs.*

When they come ashore to breed, the animals become vulnerable to disturbance by people.

Like other bottom-dwelling marine arthropods, horseshoe crabs are easily caught. In Asia they are collected for food by local people. However, while they have been used in the souvenir trade, it is their collection for industrial use, such as for making chicken food and fertilizers, that seems to have most seriously affected horseshoe crab populations.

Crane, Whooping

Grus americana

Intensive conservation efforts have pulled the whooping crane back from the brink of extinction. There is now hope that this rescue initiative is turning into a conservation success story.

In the mid-19th century the population of whooping cranes numbered between 1,300 and 1,400 birds. By 1938 heavy hunting pressure, widespread habitat conversion, and general disturbance by people had reduced the population to just 14 adults. Such a large reduction in numbers was inevitably accompanied by a huge contraction in range, and many populations became extinct.

There is now only one self-sustaining wild population, breeding in the wet prairies of Wood Buffalo National Park in central Canada. This population of 183 birds includes 50 breeding pairs and has been increasing slowly at about 5 percent per year since 1966. The major hope for the species' continuing survival rests with the wild Canadian flock.

Reintroduced Birds

A reintroduced population that includes six territorial pairs exists in Florida, but numbers are maintained by the annual introduction of more birds from captivity. However, there are hopes that the Florida population will become self-sustaining, which is not the case for the reintroduced birds in Idaho. This was an experimental flock, cross-fostered by sandhill cranes, but the birds have not reproduced.

Current Problems

Hunting and large-scale habitat loss are no longer key threats to the populations. Currently the largest known cause of death or injury to fledglings is collision with powerlines. Since overall numbers are still low, predation by golden eagles is also believed to be highly significant, especially on migration routes.

Drought is thought to be a cause of the deterioration of some breeding habitats, but availability of habitat on breeding grounds is not considered to be a limiting factor for the near future. There are more important threats, such as those affecting the major wintering site, Aransas National Wildlife Refuge in Texas. There, the risk of oil and chemical pollution is always present, along with problems related to boat traffic, wave erosion, and dredging.

DATA PANEL

Whooping crane

Grus americana

Family: Gruidae

World population: About 380 birds in the wild and captivity

Distribution: Wild population breeds in Wood Buffalo National Park, on the border of Northwest Territories and Alberta, Canada. Winters at Aransas National Wildlife Refuge, Texas. Flocks have been reintroduced to Florida and Idaho, with former nonmigratory and latter wintering south to New Mexico

Habitat: Breeds in prairie wetlands and winters in coastal brackish wetlands

Size: Length: 4.4 ft (1.3 m); wingspan: 7–8 ft (2–2.4 m). Weight: 16.5 lb (7.5 kg)

Form: Huge bird with large, horn-colored bill. Adults show black forehead, lores (area between eyes and base of bill), and "moustache," tipped red. Red crown and facial skin around bill. Black primary feathers visible in flight. Immatures whitish, with scattered brown feathers over wings and paler red-brown head and neck

Diet: In Canada snails, larval insects, leeches, frogs, minnows, small rodents, and berries; sometimes scavenges on dead ducks, marsh birds, or muskrats. During migration aquatic animals, plants roots, and waste grain in stubble fields. In Texas shellfish, snakes, acorns, small fish, and wild fruit

Breeding: Two eggs laid between late April and mid-May and incubated for about 1 month; usually only 1 fledges

Related endangered species: Include blue crane (*Grus paradisea*) VU; black-necked crane (*G. nigricollis*) VU; Siberian crane (*G. leucogeranus*) CR; wattled crane (*G. carunculatus*) VU

Status: IUCN EN; CITES I and II

Wood Buffalo National Park

CANADA

UNITED STATES

Aransas National Wildlife Refuge

MEXICO

See also: Captive Breeding 1: 87; Reintroduction 1: 92; Coot, Horned 3: 62; Kagu 5: 88

Conservation Targets

Only an intensive conservation effort has prevented the whooping crane from disappearing into extinction. Its objectives have been to maintain one self-sustaining population and to increase the captive population for further releases of birds into the wild.

The 124 captive birds are held at four main locations in Maryland, Texas, and Wisconsin in the United States, and at Calgary in Canada. In the special facilities whooping crane chicks are kept in isolation from humans. They are fed through a hole in the wall by an adult whooping crane glove puppet. Simulation of this kind is designed to make the birds' eventual introduction to the wild as successful as possible. Since the choice of migration routes, nesting locations, and wintering sites is learned rather than instinctive, the captive-breeding programs also focus on teaching birds to migrate by following light aircraft or vehicles on the ground.

The species is the subject of a transnational recovery plan, which has a number of ambitious but necessary targets. Current efforts are designed to increase the size of the existing wild population and to establish two further self-sustaining reintroduced populations. An important part of the conservation plan is to ensure that the self-sustaining populations in the wild grow to at least 1,000 birds.

The whooping crane *is a huge white crane that is threatened by the high incidence of collisions with powerlines among fledglings. A recent experiment aimed at making the lines more visible has reduced collisions by 40 to 60 percent.*

Crayfish, Noble

Astacus astacus

The noble crayfish is found in limestone streams and rivers in Europe. It is the finest species of freshwater crayfish and as such commands a high price as a luxury food. Overfishing, introduced competitors, and a fungal disease have drastically reduced its numbers.

Crayfish (or crawfish) are large crustaceans that are close relatives of lobsters. About 500 other species of crayfish are known from many parts of the world, excluding Africa (one species occurs in Madagascar), Antarctica, and northern Asia. More than half the number of known crayfish species come from North America.

Crayfish have calcareous exoskeletons, or shells. Their head and thorax are fused together into a tough carapace—the cephalothorax. The head bears paired eyes, prominent, long sensory antennae, and smaller sensory structures called antennules. The first pair of walking legs is armed with pincers or claws, which are used to collect food and for defense, and behind them are four more pairs of walking legs. Because the crayfish has 10 legs, it is called a decapod. The abdomen is made up of a number of segments that fold against each other. At the rear end is a small tail fan; and when the crayfish is alarmed, it can flick the abdomen while the fan is spread and jerk backward in a rapid escape response. The strong abdominal muscles that allow this response form the flesh of the crayfish, which is considered a delicious food.

Crayfish are active by night. They feed on a variety of aquatic plants and animals, but they are often regarded as scavengers rather than carnivores. While a few species inhabit marine environments, most live in freshwater lakes, streams, and rivers, where they often hide under rocks or logs. Some species inhabit swampy places or marshland, where they live in burrows. They provide food for various freshwater fish species and are sometimes used as bait by anglers.

Delicacy

In Europe crayfish have been considered a delicacy for centuries; and the noble crayfish, being the largest of the European freshwater crayfish species and believed to be the most delicious to eat, was at one time reserved as food for rich and powerful nobles.

Because of its popularity as a delicacy, the early settlers arriving in America from France and

DATA PANEL

Noble crayfish (noble crawfish)

Astacus astacus

Family: Astacidae

World population: Unknown

Distribution: Northern and central Europe; possibly Cyprus and Italy

Habitat: Freshwater streams, rivers, lakes, and the Baltic Sea, where salinity is very low

Size: Length: up to 5 in (12.5 cm)

Form: Lobsterlike crustacean with a fused head and thorax, flexible abdomen, antennae, front legs with powerful pincers, and 4 further pairs of walking legs

Diet: Mainly scavengers; will eat water plants and small aquatic animals

Breeding: Sexes separate. Female lays eggs (in spring) that are carried on her abdominal

appendages. Crayfish larvae hatch from the eggs in 5–8 weeks and stay attached to mother for several weeks until they are large enough to lead an independent life

Related endangered species: About 12 in the U.S., including the Tennessee cave crayfish (*Orconectes incomptus*) VU; 2 in Europe, and 24 in Australasia and the Far East

Status: IUCN VU; not listed by CITES

See also: Introductions **1:** 54; Disease **1:** 55; Crab, California Bay Pea **3:** 72

Scandinavia brought with them knowledge of freshwater crayfish, and the various American freshwater crayfish soon acquired popularity as a food.

A Deadly Disease

Unfortunately, a virulent crayfish disease was exported from the United States to Europe in consignments of American crayfish. So serious is the disease that there have been a number of attempts to ban imports of crayfish into various European countries, and the subject has been discussed by the European Commission. The disease is commonly known as the crayfish plague, and it is caused by a fungus that feeds on crayfish tissue.

It is sometimes difficult to detect infection in the early stages of the disease, but later it appears as woolly puffs of fungal threads growing from the joints of the shell on the abdomen. When infected with the fungus, the crayfish start to show changes in behavior, moving around in the daytime and appearing disorientated. Soon the plague results in the extermination of the crayfish stocks from a particular area. Unlike their American counterparts, European crayfish have been unable to develop a natural resistance to the disease.

The plague has decimated the natural populations of many of the native European crayfish. This in turn has had serious effects on the ecology of some European waterways; an important dietary component of freshwater fish has been lost, and aquatic vegetation—usually browsed on by the crayfish—has flourished out of hand. Initially an obvious solution to the problem seemed to be the importation of foreign crayfish to take their place. But this was a disaster. Not only are some of the imported crayfish more aggressive than the noble crayfish, they are also more resistant to the disease, which they harbor as a hidden infection, to be spread further as they move around. The importation and movement of crayfish need to be strictly controlled to prevent the disease from spreading further.

The noble crayfish *has a segmented body, a thin, tough exoskeleton, and eyes on movable stalks. The large front pair of legs are armed with powerful pincers.*

Crocodile, American

Crocodylus acutus

The American crocodile has a much wider distribution than the American alligator. Although in the United States it is restricted to southern Florida, it is found in 16 other countries. Like the alligator, it has been hunted to supply the lucrative trade in leather made from crocodile skin.

In the United States crocodiles live in the tidal marshes in the Everglades along Florida Bay and in the Florida Keys. The American crocodile is also found in western Mexico through Central America down to northeastern Peru and into Venezuela. It occurs on some Caribbean islands, mainly Cuba (which has the largest wild population) and also Jamaica, Haiti, and the Dominican Republic. In all these countries crocodile populations have declined.

Crocodiles are fairly adaptable; they are excellent swimmers, they can travel considerable distances overland, and they can live in fresh or salt water. However, urban development—for example in Dade and Monroe counties, Florida—has reduced their habitat. One population has taken refuge in brackish water cooling channels at Turkey Point nuclear power station in Florida.

Like alligators, crocodiles do not usually attack humans unless they or their nests are disturbed. In Florida the crocodiles and their nests are strictly protected; killing, feeding, or disturbing them in any way is illegal.

Crocodiles are good burrowers, excavating deep holes for shelter and nesting. In the absence of suitable soil they will cover the eggs with a mound of loose vegetation. Eggs and youngsters are vulnerable to predators. Racoons in the United States dig up their nests, as do teiid lizards in Central America. Flooding can also destroy nests before the eggs hatch.

Souvenir Hunt

The American crocodile is threatened both by urban development and by other forms of habitat destruction. In Ecuador, for example, mangroves have been cleared for shrimp aquaculture. Crocodiles are also sometimes killed out of fear or because they are seen as a threat to

---

DATA PANEL

American crocodile

Crocodylus acutus

Family: Crocodylidae

World population: Unknown

Distribution: Southern Florida, Central America, Peru, and Venezuela

Habitat: Fresh and salt water; swamps, rivers, lakes, reservoirs, and mangrove swamps

Size: Length: male 16–19 ft (5–6 m); female up to 16 ft (5 m). Reports of specimens 22 ft (7 m) long in Central America. Weight: 700–800 lb (318–363 kg)

Form: Large lizardlike reptiles with longer and narrower snouts than alligators and a body that is not as well armored. The fourth tooth on each side of the lower jaw is visible when the mouth is closed. Coloration is green-gray or gray-tan with dusky markings. Adults have a prominent swelling in front of each eye

Diet: Fish, crabs, turtles, birds, and small mammals; can attack livestock

Breeding: Clutches of 20–60 eggs are laid in excavated holes or buried in mounds of loose vegetation. Incubation takes about 3 months

Related endangered species: Orinoco crocodile (*Crocodylus intermedius*) CR; Philippines crocodile (*C. mindorensis*) CR; marsh or mugger crocodile (*C. palustris*) VU; Cuban crocodile (*C. rhombifer*) EN; Siamese crocodile (*C. siamensis*) CR

Status: IUCN VU; CITES I

UNITED STATES
MEXICO
BAHAMAS
CUBA
NICARAGUA
VENEZUELA
COLUMBIA
ECUADOR
BRAZIL
PERU

See also: Organizations **1:** 10; Alligator, American **2:** 10; Gharial **5:** 24

livestock. Illegal hunting for
the trade in skins or for making
tourist souvenirs is common. Other threats include
accidental capture in fishing nets, tropical storms, and
overfishing; fish form a large part of their diet.

Conservation

The Crocodile Specialist Group (CSG) consists of
experts and other interested parties who advise the
Species Survival Commission of the IUCN on
crocodilian conservation. Operating from the Florida
Museum of Natural History, the group monitors
crocodile populations and draws up conservation
programs; by 1971 the CSG had set up a conservation
program for all 23 crocodilian species throughout the
world. Monitoring the crocodiles is a mammoth task.
The most detailed study has been that of the Florida
population, but in several countries very little up-to-
date information is available, and there is a need for
more fieldwork. The CSG is funded by voluntary
donations, so funds are not always sufficient to do
what is needed.

The American crocodile *feeds in the water (often
floating at the surface to lie in wait for prey) and comes onto
land to bask in the sun and to lay eggs.*

The American crocodile was listed as Endangered
in 1979, and a recovery plan was initiated by the
United States Fish and Wildlife Service in 1984 to
cover aspects such as habitat protection and captive-
breeding programs. Captive breeding for the skin
trade and restocking exists in six countries, but recent
reduced demand for skins may remove the financial
incentive for this to continue. Few zoos have captive-
breeding programs, although one notable success was
the hatching of 10 young crocodiles in 1996 at
Cleveland Metroparks Zoo. In Venezuela protection
and releases of captive-bred stock are aiding recovery.

Florida's crocodile population is slowly increasing,
but in several countries (such as El Salvador and Haiti)
they are still declining. There is an urgent need for
restocking of the wild populations.

Crow, Hawaiian

Corvus hawaiiensis

One of the world's rarest birds, the Hawaiian crow has a minute population of just three birds. Unless conservationists can augment the wild population with captive-bred birds and their offspring, the species is doomed to extinction in the very near future.

With its minuscule present-day population, it is hard to believe that the Hawaiian crow—or alala—was once quite widespread and common on Hawaii, the main island of the Hawaiian Island group in the Pacific. It is the only representative of the crow family to have reached the island group in "recent" times, but other species are known from the islands' fossil record. It is likely that its range was always restricted to the island of Hawaii, although there is no obvious reason for this.

Change of Fortune

The Hawaiian crow was once described by an American ornithologist as extremely numerous in some areas of the island. Yet before the end of the 19th century the same observer, along with other ornithologists, had commented on the decrease in the crow's population and described the species' restricted range as "an unsolved enigma."

It is known that in the late 19th century native Hawaiians were still snaring the crows and using their blackish-brown feathers for decoration and for dressing idols. However, this is unlikely to have had a major effect on the crow population—contrasting with the war waged on the birds by farmers, including an orchestrated shooting campaign in the Kona region in the 1890s. Shooting (as well as collection for taxidermy) is likely to have had a serious effect on the numbers of the birds and, despite being illegal since 1931, continued to a certain extent until recently, when the species was given complete protection.

Another major problem—one that has devastated populations of many other Hawaiian birds—is the massive scale of habitat alteration. The ohia-koa forest

DATA PANEL

Hawaiian crow (alala)

Corvus hawaiiensis

Family: Corvidae

World population: Three birds

Distribution: Found only on the island of Hawaii; today survives only in the Kona Forest Unit of the Hakalau National Wildlife Refuge

Habitat: Wet ohia-koa forest, scrub, and rangelands; now more or less restricted to high mountain forest

Size: Length: 19–19.8 in (48–50 cm)

Form: Large crow with dark plumage—dull, sooty brown, with paler brown primary wingtip feathers; dark-brown eyes; heavy black bill, and strong black legs; juveniles have blue eyes and pink lining to mouth

Diet: Omnivorous: feeds mainly on fruit and berries of native shrubs and plants in the forest understory; also eats spiders and isopod crustaceans

Breeding: Solitary nester; bulky nest of branches and sticks is lined with soft grasses and plant stems; often sited in isolated stands of tall trees next to more open habitat; nests apparently used over many years by successive generations of birds; lays 5 eggs in late April; incubation by both sexes (unusual for crows)

Related endangered species: Five other species of crow are threatened: Banggai crow (*Corvus unicolor*) EN; Cuban palm crow (*C. minutus*) EN; Flores crow (*C. florensis*) EN; Mariana crow (*C. kubaryi*) EN; white-necked crow (*C. leucognaphalus*) VU. In addition, 2 crows are LRnt, and several jays, magpies, and other relatives in the crow family are EN

Status: IUCN CR; not listed by CITES

Kauai
Oahu
Hawaii
(UNITED STATES)
Maui
Hawaii
Hakalau National
Wildlife Refuge

See also: Habitat Loss **1:** 38; Captive Breeding **1:** 87; Blackbird, Saffron-Cowled **2:** 92; Nene **7:** 10

has been degraded and fragmented by commercial logging and the conversion of forest to agricultural land. Introduced grazing animals, as well as logging and agricultural operations, destroy the plants of the understory (on which the crows depend for food) and are factors in the disappearance of species that pollinate and disperse such plants. A further threat is from fire and the subsequent invasion of the fire-adapted fountain-grass and fire tree.

Other known threats include the plundering of flightless young crows by two introduced predators, the black rat and small Indian mongoose, as well as predation by the Hawaiian hawk. In addition, the crows have suffered from the avian malaria and viral pox that are transmitted by mosquitoes, originally introduced to the islands by sailors in the 1820s. This may be a factor in the crow's present restricted range, since mosquitoes do not live above medium altitudes, although forest destruction and shooting have been more significant in its decline.

Risk of Extinction

By the mid-1970s the population of Hawaiian crows had fallen to about 70 individuals, and a captive-breeding program was started. By late 1999, after further declines, just three birds remained in the wild,

The Hawaiian crow, *regarded by native Hawaiians as an* aumakua, *or guardian spirit, could soon be extinct after long-term habitat destruction and poor breeding success.*

including a pair probably no longer able to reproduce. Breeding failure dogged the dwindling population for many years, with complete failure common.

The captive-breeding facility did not have much success. Developed for the threatened nene (Hawaiian goose), it was originally in unsuitable habitat. Despite a move to a more suitable site, 18 of the 24 captive-bred birds released by 1998 were found to have died. The remaining captive-bred birds were taken into care in an attempt to preserve the species' genetic diversity. In September 1998, after three birds died in as many days, the release program was stopped.

The conservation team has several urgent aims; but whatever is achieved, unless captive-bred birds and their offspring can survive to augment the wild population, the Hawaiian crow could soon be extinct.

Curlew, Eskimo

Numenius borealis

A once numerous species, the Eskimo curlew is perhaps already extinct. Large declines in the 19th century left very few birds, and since the mid-1980s there have been only unconfirmed reports of its existence.

The Eskimo curlew probably once had a population of hundreds of thousands, but it declined suddenly between the 1870s and 1890s. Sightings during the first half of the 20th century were rare, and since 1945 the most frequent reports have come from Texas, a point on the bird's return migration from South America. The last confirmed sighting in South America was in 1939, but there have been no confirmed sightings anywhere at all since 1985.

However, there have been a number of reported sightings of the Eskimo curlew—in 1987 (Texas), in 1990 (Argentina), several during the early 1990s (United States), and in 1996 (Prairie Provinces, Canada)—but none of these have been confirmed. Additional reported discoveries of breeding birds are unsubstantiated or have been shown to refer to closely related or similar-looking species.

Widespread Searches

It is not unknown for species in the Americas that were thought to be extinct or nearing extinction to be rediscovered in reasonable numbers. They include, among others, the austral rail in Argentina, the black-hooded antwren in Brazil, and the brown-banded antpitta in Colombia. Unfortunately, such discoveries are unlikely in the case of the Eskimo curlew.

Nonetheless, there have been a number of specific initiatives to help improve the quality of reported sightings from certain areas, including the prairies and the east coast of North America. For example, all aspects of the Eskimo curlew's status and ecology

last known range

last known range

DATA PANEL

Eskimo curlew

Numenius borealis

Family: Scolopacidae

World population: Possibly extinct; if it still survives, the population is tiny

Distribution: Was known to breed at 2 locations in Northwest Territories, Canada. Migrates across Hudson Bay to Labrador and New England, then flies south across Caribbean to northeastern Argentina. Return migration thought to be up Pacific coast of South America, through Central America, and across Gulf of Mexico; birds land on Texas coast before drifting northward to the breeding sites

Habitat: Breeds in the treeless arctic tundra, migrating through heathlands, pastures, and intertidal flats. Winters in wet grasslands, intertidal habitats, and semidesert. Return migration in North America is through tallgrass and mixed-grass prairies

Size: Length: 11.5–13.5 in (29–34 cm); wingspan: 32–33.5 in (81–85 cm). Weight: 9.5–16 oz (270–454 g)

Form: Small, cinnamon-colored bird with downcurved bill; larger and shorter-legged than little curlew and 25% smaller than whimbrel. Wings extend beyond tip of tail; cinnamon below, with heavily barred breast and Y-shaped marks on flanks

Diet: In Northwest Territories ants, grubs, freshwater insects, and crowberries. During migration: on rocky coastlines snails, worms, and other invertebrates; in uplands mainly crowberries; south of crowberry range and in Argentina insects. On return migration in North American prairies, diet included the now extinct Rocky Mountain grasshopper

Breeding: Four eggs laid May–August

Related endangered species: Bristle-thighed curlew (*Numenius tahitiensis*) VU; Far-Eastern curlew (*N. madagascariensis*) LRnt; long-billed curlew (*N. americanus*) LRnt; slender-billed curlew (*N. tenuirostris*) CR

Status: IUCN CR; CITES I

See also: Organizations 1: 10; Communities and Ecosystems 1: 22; Plover, Piping 7: 84

have been documented, and detailed information has been provided to ornithologists about identification. Previously known breeding areas have also been extensively surveyed, and teams of biologists have followed up all reported breeding sites.

Extensive surveys of suitable habitat for wintering grounds in Argentina and Uruguay between 1992 and 1993 failed to find any birds. Added to the intensive search efforts, the reasons behind the decline of the Eskimo curlew suggest that even if there are a few birds left, they are unlikely to persist for long.

An important contributory factor to the decline in population during the second half of the 19th century is known to have been the hunting of large numbers along spring migratory pathways in North America. Hunting alone has often been used to explain the species' decline to near extinction. However, after hunting was outlawed and finally abandoned in 1916, no recovery took place.

Another factor is now thought to be a prime reason for the Eskimo curlew's decline: the near total loss of the North American tallgrass prairie ecosystem to agriculture during the late 19th century. Habitat conversion was combined with the deliberate suppression of prairie wildfires and therefore led to a reduction in the number of recently burned areas preferred by the Eskimo curlew. Also of significance was the extinction of a key prairie food source for the Eskimo curlew: the Rocky Mountain grasshopper.

The Eskimo curlew *once existed in large numbers. It may now be extinct as a result of hunting and habitat destruction.*

An Important Lesson

The Canadian Recovery Team remains officially on hold awaiting proof of the species' continuing existence or the discovery of a remnant population. However, even if the Eskimo curlew is already extinct, it has left an important message about the need to manage prairie habitat for wildlife as well as food production. There are several other globally threatened birds in the prairies, such as the lesser prairie chicken and Sprague's pipit. The conservation of native prairie habitat is essential if other species are not to go the same way as the Eskimo curlew.

85

Cuscus, Black-Spotted

Spilocuscus rufoniger

The black-spotted cuscus is a marsupial mammal found only on the island of New Guinea. Few have ever been seen by scientists, and virtually nothing is known about their ecology.

Cuscuses are furry marsupials that belong to the same family as possums. There are 18 species in all, of which nine are currently considered to be at risk. The black-spotted cuscus is one of the largest and rarest of these animals. Records of living specimens are so few that much of what is written about the species is based on observations of its close relatives or else on anecdotes.

Remote and Little Known

The earliest account of a black-spotted cuscus dates back to 1936. Expeditions in the 1980s and 1990s yielded a few more details about the species' physiology, but very little was learned about their way of life. In the intervening years local people have continued to hunt black-spotted cuscuses with some success, and the hunters claim to know some details of the animal's behavior. The

cuscus seems to be mostly nocturnal and arboreal, although it is probably capable of bounding along the ground if necessary. It is said to eat mostly tree seeds, but is probably an omnivore like its relatives, taking advantage of whatever food is available.

Trade in any of the spotted cuscuses is restricted under CITES regulations, but these do not prevent local people from shooting the animals for their meat. The black-spotted cuscus is clearly much rarer than its close relative, the spotted cuscus, which is itself widely hunted by the native peoples of New Guinea. Yet the members of at least one tribe nonetheless insist that the *tekeib*, as they call the black-spotted cuscus, is really extremely common, even though it is hardly ever captured or killed. They explain this paradox by claiming that the animal has mystical powers that prevent it from being caught by any hunter who has not prepared himself with various magical rituals.

In a sample of cuscus jaw bones collected by native hunters, fewer than 15 percent came from

DATA PANEL

Black-spotted cuscus

Spilocuscus rufoniger (Phalanger atrimaculatus, P. maculatus rufoniger)

Family: Phalangeridae

World population: Unknown, but certainly very small

Distribution: Northern New Guinea

Habitat: Forests from sea level to 4,000 ft (1,200 m)

Size: Length head/body: 22–25 in (58–64 cm); measurements based on only 2 specimens, female larger. Weight: 12–14 lb (5.5–6.6 kg); measurements based on 3 specimens

Form: Tree-living animal with long, thick tail and short legs; rounded head with large, round eyes and small, furry ears; fur dense and woolly; male is red with black spots, female pale brown with dark saddle patch

Diet: Unknown; may include nuts, leaves, fruit, and flowers; possibly also insects and meat (such as birds and lizards) when found

Breeding: Unknown; probably 1 young, carried in pouch until well developed

Related endangered species: Obi Island cuscus (*Phalanger rothschildi*) VU; Stein's cuscus (*P. vestitus*) VU; Telefomin cuscus (*P. matanim*) EN

Status: IUCN EN; not listed by CITES

See also: Superstition 1: 47; Possum, Leadbeater's 7: 88; Tree-Kangaroo, Goodfellow's 10: 4

black-spotted cuscuses. Nevertheless, the fact that the species continues to turn up from time to time is cause for some optimism. It may be that the black-spotted cuscus is capable of surviving at low population densities or simply lives in places where hunters and scientists rarely manage to find it. But such scenarios offer at best a slim hope, and most experts fear that the animal will disappear altogether before long. The risk is difficult to calculate because so little is known about the animal.

Long-Range Forecast

Black-spotted cuscuses live only in dense, undisturbed forest. At one time this choice of habitat kept the species relatively secure, since hunters rarely attempted to pursue animals into such terrain, where spears and arrows are of little use. Since the late 1960s, however, the use of firearms, especially shotguns, has taken a severe toll on all the region's wildlife. Although rare, the black-spotted cuscus makes an easy target once it has been spotted, since the brightly colored fur of the

Black-spotted cuscuses *are shy, nocturnal animals that are prized for their coats in their native New Guinea. The spots from which the species takes its name are present in the male, but the female (above) is plain pale brown.*

male, combined with its habit of sleeping on high, exposed branches during the day, makes it highly visible, even from a distance. It is no coincidence that the only places where the species appears to survive today are those with small human populations and a limited availability of guns and ammunition.

Sadly for the black-spotted cuscus, areas with small human populations are few and far between, and for the most part such areas are not protected. Logging and subsistence agriculture are also destroying the forests at an alarming rate. The cuscus is not able to tolerate disturbance of its habitat and apparently does not recolonize forest that regenerates after the original trees have been cleared. In other words, once the species has disappeared from an area, it is unlikely to return.

Cushion Star

Asterina phylactica

The cushion star was not identified as a separate species until 1979. Previously it had been classified with the gibbous starlet, a slightly larger starfish that lacks the conspicuous darker star pattern found on the upper surface of the cushion star.

Cushion stars are starfish (sea stars) with five thick, short arms. Starfish are themselves not fish, but echnoderms: spiny-skinned marine invertebrates of the class Asteroidea, and they are different from most other types of animal. Their bodies are star-shaped with (usually five) rays, or arms, surrounding an indistinct disk. They have no brain and no obvious eyes or other conspicuous sense organs. The lack of eyes and other sensory equipment does not mean that they cannot detect stimuli such as touch, chemicals, or light. In fact, the outer surface of a starfish plays an important role in detecting predators and food. The body is covered with spines and microscopic grooming organs that resemble minute forceps or tongs.

The mouth is situated on the underside of the body; the intestine rises up through the center of the animal with a digestive pocket branching out into each of the five rays.

Under the starfish's rays are grooves with rows of feet tipped by suckers that help them grip rocks and manipulate prey. Most species of starfish feed on small animals such as worms and crustaceans. The prey are either manipulated whole into the mouth using the tube feet or eaten—remarkably—by extending the stomach out through the mouth, wrapping it around the victim, and digesting it outside the starfish body.

Scientists did not recognize the cushion star as a distinct species of starfish until 1979. Before then it was classified with the gibbous starlet *Asterina gibbosa* because of its similar size and appearance. The cushion star is slightly smaller and has a conspicuous darker star pattern on its upper surface.

Crucial Stages of Growth

Typically, starfish are dioecious (sexes are separate). Some, however, are hermaphrodites (having both male and female reproductive organs) and pass through a male phase before becoming females. Some species brood (sit on, or hatch) their eggs in a process that is similar to the the brooding of birds, except that no heat is transferred; others release the eggs into the water where they are fertilized externally.

Both the cushion star and gibbous starlet are hermaphrodites, and both lay eggs attached to the rocks. However, while the gibbous starlet abandons its eggs after they have been laid, the cushion star stays with its eggs and broods them.

DATA PANEL

Cushion star

Asterina phylactica

Family: Echinidae

World population: Unknown

Distribution: Mediterranean Sea and northeastern Atlantic

Habitat: Rock pools and shallow water down to 66 ft (20 m)

Size: Up to 0.6 in (1.5 cm) across

Form: Typical starfish form with 5 short rays (arms); body surface covered with short spines. On underside grooves contain rows of tube feet tipped with suckers

Diet: Small animals such as worms and crustaceans

Breeding: Adults are hermaphrodites (having both male and female organs). Eggs are laid on rocks and brooded by parent until they metamorphose into juveniles

Related endangered species: None

Status: Not listed by IUCN; not listed by CITES

See also: Pollution 1: 50; Sea Anemone, Starlet 8: 58; Sea-Urchin, Edible 8: 66

The cushion star *on a rocky shore; suckers on the feet help it cling to the rock. Respiration takes place through structures in the skin.*

Unusually, there is no larval phase in the cushion star and gibbous starlet. In the majority of starfish fertilized eggs develop into larvae, which join the community of plankton—floating plants and animals that are suspended in the surface waters and move by means of the currents rather than by active swimming. (Plankton means "drifting" in Greek.) There they feed on minute planktonic plants before metamorphosis occurs. The larval stage allows the distribution of the species around the world's seas, avoids competition with the adults for food and living space in one area, and ensures a healthy mixing of genetic material.

Vulnerable on Two Counts

Because their life cycles lack a planktonic larval phase, the gibbous starlet and cushion star cannot disperse their young widely. As a result, the adult populations are not well mixed genetically and are therefore more vulnerable as a species. According to the extent of their geographical isolation, they may evolve into different races or even into new species.

The cushion star has not yet been placed on the IUCN Red Data List, but it is a suitable candidate. Its distribution in northwestern Europe and the Mediterranean Sea is local and patchy.

Evidence shows that the cushion star is vulnerable to oil pollution. A recent oil spillage in Wales seriously reduced the population because it depends on clean rocks to brood its young after the eggs have been laid. Furthermore, when the oil killed off the adults, there were no planktonic larvae to recolonize the area.

Dace, Mountain Blackside

Phoxinus cumberlandensis

Restricted to a few streams in the Cumberland River drainage system in Kentucky and northeastern Tennessee, the mountain blackside dace is threatened on several fronts. Habitat alteration as a direct result of logging, mining, and road construction has contributed to competition with other species and resulted in reduced populations.

The first specimens of the mountain blackside dace were collected in 1975 within the Daniel Boone National Forest. Because they were colored the same as other *Phoxinus* species, little attention was paid to the specimens, although they came from a small area where dace populations had not been studied before. It took three more years for the differences between the mountain blackside dace and its closest relatives to be fully appreciated. Since then a great deal has been learned about the fish.

Silt-Sensitive

Of particular interest is the mountain blackside dace's sensitivity to silt-laden water, a characteristic that restricts it to clear-water areas of streams—especially pools of about 39 inches (100 cm) depth—fed by flowing water from narrower, shallower stretches. Such pools contain undercut banks and dense surrounding vegetation. The substratum can be sandy, gravelly, or rocky, but is free of fine sediments. Most pools are located at altitudes of about 900 to 1,600 feet (275 to 490 m) above sea level.

The mountain blackside dace exhibits coloration like that of several other species in the genus *Phoxinus*, in which the males in particular display brilliantly during the breeding season.

Short-Stretch Distribution

Although no proof is available at the moment, there is a possibility that in the past the mountain blackside dace may have occurred in well over 50 other streams within the Cumberland River system. Populations are currently only known from about 30 streams in the upper reaches of the system. In addition, of the known populations 27 are restricted to stretches of water of about 1 mile (1.5 km) or less. Some are actually found within stretches of only a few hundred yards. The mountain blackside dace must be considered significantly at risk, since all the streams are located within a relatively small area and so could be altered by the same environmental factors.

DATA PANEL

Mountain blackside dace

Phoxinus cumberlandensis

Family: Cyprinidae

World population: Unknown

Distribution: Short stretches of streams in Cumberland River drainage system of southeastern Kentucky and northeastern Tennessee

Habitat: Silt-free pools in upper reaches of streams where there is a flow of cool running water. Substratum of sand, gravel, pebbles, and rocks. Undercut banks, particularly shaded by overlapping vegetation

Size: Length: 2.8 in (7.2 cm)

Form: Slim-bodied fish with pointed snout and short, robust fins. Black stripe runs from snout, through eye, and along body, ending at caudal peduncle (base of tail). In mature male the chin/throat area, "neck," and whole of underside of body are red,

especially during breeding season. Base of dorsal (back) fin is also red. Rest of fins are dusky gold or yellow, while top half of body is olive gold

Diet: Mainly algae, detritus, and small aquatic invertebrates

Breeding: In April–June males gather at silt-free nest sites and await the arrival of a female. When one arrives, groups of males swarm around her and spawn with her. Little else is known, but the young are believed to mature in 1 year. Life span between 3 and 4 years

Related endangered species: Tennessee dace *(Phoxinus tennesseensis)* LRnt

Status: IUCN VU; not listed by CITES

Illinois | Indiana | Ohio | West Virginia | Kentucky | Virginia | Tennessee | North Carolina | UNITED STATES | South Carolina | Alabama | Georgia

See also: Pollution **1:** 50; Danio, Barred **3:** 94; Ikan Temoleh **5:** 82; Shark, Silver **8:** 84; Sucker, Razorback **9:** 38

Few species of fish apart from the mountain blackside dace are found in these waters. However, one that is sometimes encountered is the southern redbelly dace. An interesting relationship exists between the two species with dominance seemingly determined by water flow. Where water flow is relatively high, resulting in clear, sediment-free water, the mountain blackside dace tends to outnumber its relative. However, where this flow has been reduced—for example, by alteration of the stream gradient—the southern redbelly assumes dominance, sometimes to the extent that it totally replaces the mountain blackside dace over a period of time.

This dynamic relationship was discovered not long after the mountain blackside dace was recognized as a separate species. It provided a clear early warning signal that the species could be placed under serious threat by a competitor that was able to exploit slow-water conditions to its advantage.

Decline and Recovery

The main problem facing the mountain blackside dace is changes in ambient conditions—which can include a rise in water temperature—to favor the southern redbelly dace. The higher suspended silt content of the water in altered habitats is obviously significant. As a consequence, the southern redbelly—along with other species like the bluntnose minnow—not only finds a foothold alongside the mountain blackside dace, but also competes with it for available food resources.

A further threat comes from coal mines in the area. Strip mining in particular has resulted in heavy siltation, as well as acidic runoff, and the two factors together have caused declines in the mountain blackside dace populations in affected streams. Whether or not modern coal-mining techniques are still having the same effect is not clear at the moment.

Logging, road construction, and other habitat-altering activities within the species' range have also had (and are still having) a negative effect on population levels. A study carried out in the mid-1980s indicated that the combined effects of all these factors had led to a situation where only nine of the 30 known habitats contained healthy mountain blackside dace populations.

To what extent, if any, the species has recovered or declined further in the locations in recent years is not known. The key to its survival in its native waters undoubtedly lies in adequate monitoring and control of the habitat-altering and habitat-degrading factors that so easily affect its populations.

Mountain blackside dace *exhibit colors like their relatives'—red, black, white or silver, and dusky gold.*

Damselfly, Southern

Coenagrion mercuriale

Damselflies and their close relatives the dragonflies are familiar waterside insects that hunt their prey on the wing. The drainage of ponds and marshes for agriculture and urban development—as well as an increase in the use of pesticides—threatens to wipe out these beautiful insects.

The brilliantly colored southern damselfly frequents sluggish streams in lowland areas. In Britain it is restricted to a handful of counties such as Hampshire and Dorset in the south of the country. It is more widely distributed across northwestern Europe, from France and Germany southward to the Mediterranean. Southern damselflies are also known to exist in North Africa.

Damselflies and dragonflies are familiar pond and streamside insects. Both have long, slender bodies, keen eyesight, and two pairs of wings. However, it is not difficult to tell the two insects apart. Damselflies are generally smaller and slimmer than their close relatives. In dragonflies the front wings and hind wings are of different shapes, with the hind wings being generally broader. In damselflies the wings are the same shape and taper into a narrow stalk just before they join the body. The two types of insect also alight and rest differently. Dragonflies always rest with their wings outspread, while damselflies perch with their wings only partly spread or held vertically over the body.

The southern damselfly is a day-flying insect, and eyesight is important in all its activities. In many cases the eyes are so large that the head appears to consist of little else. However, damselfly eyes are not quite as dominant as those of the dragonfly and are set farther apart, making the front end of the animal look slightly hammer shaped. Since the head can swivel on the neck, the insects have almost 360-degree vision.

Correspondingly, the senses of smell and touch are less well developed. The jaws are well equipped for biting and strongly toothed, a fact reflected in the name of the order: Odonata, meaning "toothed." The damselfiles are harmless to humans, but feed on a variety of small insects such as mosquitoes and small flies, which they hunt down on the wing.

Reproduction

The reproductive lives of southern damselflies are closely connected with the water by which they live. The long, slender abdomen of the male is equipped with a pair of claspers situated near its rear tip. Just in front of the claspers are the openings of the male reproductive organs. When preparing to mate, the male transfers a drop of sperm from the

DATA PANEL

Southern damselfly

Coenagrion mercuriale

Family: Coenagrionidae

World population: Unknown

Distribution: Southern Britain; northwestern Europe from France and Germany southward to the Mediterranean; North Africa

Habitat: Slow-running streams and boggy ground

Size: Length: 0.9–1.2 in (2.4–2.7 cm); wingspan: 1–1.4 in (2.5–3.5 cm)

Form: Resembles small dragonfly; long, slim, brilliantly colored body; conspicuous eyes; 2 pairs of wings

Diet: Adults feed on small insects, including mosquitoes; nymphs (larvae) feed on small aquatic animals such as other insect larvae

Breeding: Males go in search of females in spring. After courtship and copulation eggs laid under water in water plants. Free-living larvae hatch and may feed for many weeks before emerging to molt as adult damselflies

Related endangered species: Several, including Frey's damselfly (*Coenagrion hylas freyi*) CR

Status: IUCN VU; not listed by CITES

See also: Communities and Ecosystems 1: 22; Saving the Habitats 1: 88; Emerald, Orange-Spotted 4: 70

opening by bending his abdomen forward and underneath to touch special receptacles near the front of the abdomen (just behind the last pair of walking legs). He then flies off to find a female to mate with and takes hold of her by the neck using his claspers. Mating is then achieved as the male perches holding the female while she bends her abdomen around under his body to touch her tip against his sperm-filled receptacles. She then takes some sperm into her reproductive tract. After mating, the pair may fly around in the "tandem" position, with the male towing the female; this may often be observed in the spring. The female damselfly then dips the tip of her abdomen in the water to touch a suitable water plant. She makes a small cut with her egg-laying appendage and deposits her eggs in the plant tissue.

The eggs hatch into an aquatic larvae known as nymphs. The larvae live in the water and breathe by means of gills carried on three tail projections at the tip of the abdomen. Like adults, the nymphs are carnivores and hunt for aquatic food, small worms, and the larvae of other insects. They have a specially adapted set of mouthparts called the mask. It is normally kept folded under the head, but can be extended with great speed, effectively spearing the victim on the terminal clawlike extensions.

The southern damselfly's *brilliant coloration is due to pigments and the optical properties of the outer layer of the body.*

Conflict over Conservation

Because of its rarity the southern damselfly has recently become the subject of government-sponsored conservation efforts in Britain. Plans are in progress to allow swiftly flowing trout streams and the well-drained land associated with them to deteriorate naturally into habitat that is more suitable for the endangered southern damselfly, namely slower-running waters with boggy ground and soft banks.

The proposals have given rise to conflict between the trout-fishing lobby and conservationists, but this has only served to highlight the needs of the southern damselfly. It is difficult to convince some people of the need to protect the damselfly, but slow progress is being made.

Danio, Barred

Danio pathirana

The colorful barred danio is found only in one small river basin in southwestern Sri Lanka. Although it occurs in large numbers within its range, there is still good reason for it to be classified as Criticallly Endangered. A single natural or man-made disaster could severely deplete numbers. A program of captive breeding is therefore underway that should safeguard the future of the species.

The barred danio is a brightly colored fish that belongs to a small group of species known collectively as danios. The danios have been popular aquarium fish for many years. The most well known is the zebra danio, which was first imported for aquaria in the early 1900s. It is now bred commercially in a number of color and finnage variations. Three other danios—the giant danio, the bengal danio, and a second giant danio—are also popular among aquarists and, like the zebra danio, are bred in large numbers in captivity.

Unlike other danios, the barred danio has a tiny natural range. It is restricted to just one small area of the Nilwala River Basin in southwest Sri Lanka. A potential risk for the species is that its range falls inside that of the widely distributed giant danio. Despite the overlap, the giant danio has not yet been discovered in any of the waters where the barred danio is known to exist.

The apparent absense of the giant danio is in the barred danio's favor since any form of competition or pressure, either natural (from other fish) or external (from people), would represent a serious threat to its survival. In addition, where closely related species occur together in the wild, another threat arises: potential hybridization or interbreeding. It is not known whether such a threat would exist between the two danio species since their genetic closeness has not been determined, but it is, nevertheless, a factor that should be considered if any giant danios are ever detected in barred danio waters.

Preferred Habitat

Within its native habitat the barred danio occurs in considerable numbers in streams that have a pebble or boulder substratum. It is rarely found over sand and has not been seen in the silt-bottomed tributaries that feed the main streams. Groups of between three and five individuals are typically found swimming close to the surface and in a wide variety of water conditions, ranging from fast-flowing stretches to standing pools.

In aquaria the barred danio has proved quite hardy and easy to keep. Although it has been repeatedly bred in

DATA PANEL

Barred danio

Danio pathirana

Family: Cyprinidae

World population: Unknown

Distribution: Restricted to Opatha area of Nilwala River Basin in southwestern Sri Lanka

Habitat: Wide range of water conditions; mainly habitats with pebble or rock substratum. Prefers upper layers of water column

Size: Length: 2.4 in (6 cm)

Form: Elongated, compressed body; the eyes are large, and there are 2 pairs of barbels (whiskers); 7–11 irregular metallic blue bars on the side of the body; silvery belly and blue stripe on the caudal (tail) fin

Diet: In wild, insects and other small invertebrates. Wide range of commercial formulations in aquaria

Breeding: Egg-scattering species with appetite for own eggs. Hatching takes about 4 days, with fry (newborns) becoming free-swimming a few days later

Related endangered species: Many other cyprinids

Status: IUCN CR; not listed by CITES

INDIA

SRI LANKA

Nilwala River Basin

See also: Captive Breeding **1:** 87; Barb, Bandula **2:** 52; Rasbora, Vateria Flower **8:** 22

captivity, until recently, its spawning behavior had neither been observed nor reported. However, Ananda Pathirana—the man after whom the species was named—began observing and breeding the species in captivity in the late 1990s. He reports it to be prolific and, like the other danios, an egg scatterer with a distinct appetite for its own spawn.

Holding Back

In view of the restricted nature of its distribution the barred danio was classified as Vulnerable by the IUCN in 1994, only four years after its original scientific description (it is now Critically Endangered). Despite its abundance within its range, the ornamental fish exporters of Sri Lanka voluntarily agreed with the government and conservation bodies not to collect barred danios from the wild until the species was better understood and could be bred commercially. Captive

breeding for commercial purposes has now been achieved. As a result, barred danios are now being exported—under government quota and license plans—for the worldwide aquarium market. In terms of pressure from people, therefore, the future of the barred danio seems reasonably safe. Less predictable are man-made disasters such as those caused by pollution. Another potential hazard is the effects of land alteration resulting in disruption of water courses.

The barred danio *is a favorite among aquarists because of its bright, glowing colors and high success rate in captivity. For fish with such a small natural range, captive-bred stock are a useful backup.*

Glossary

Words in SMALL CAPITALS refer to other entries in the glossary.

Adaptation features of an animal that adjust it to its environment; may be produced by evolution—e.g., camouflage coloration

Adaptive radiation where a group of closely related animals (e.g., members of a FAMILY) have evolved differences from each other so that they can survive in different NICHES

Adhesive disks flattened disks on the tips of the fingers or toes of certain climbing AMPHIBIANS that enable them to cling to smooth, vertical surfaces

Adult a fully grown sexually mature animal; a bird in its final PLUMAGE

Algae primitive plants ranging from microscopic, single-celled forms to large forms, such as seaweeds, but lacking proper roots or leaves

Alpine living in mountainous areas, usually over 5,000 feet (1,500 m)

Ambient describing the conditions around an animal, e.g., the water temperature for a fish or the air temperature for a land animal

Amphibian any cold-blooded VERTEBRATE of the CLASS Amphibia, typically living on land but breathing in the water; e.g., frogs, toads, newts, salamanders

Amphibious able to live on both land and in water

Amphipod a type of CRUSTACEAN found on land and in both fresh and seawater

Anadromous fish that spend most of their life at sea but MIGRATE into fresh water for breeding, e.g., salmon

Annelid of the PHYLUM Annelida in which the body is made up of similar segments, e.g., earthworms, lugworms, leeches

Anterior the front part of an animal

Arachnid one of a group of ARTHROPODS of the CLASS Arachnida, characterized by simple eyes and four pairs of legs. Includes spiders and scorpions

Arboreal living in trees

Aristotle's lantern complex chewing apparatus of sea-urchins that includes five teeth

Arthropod the largest PHYLUM in the animal kingdom in terms of the number of SPECIES in it. Characterized by a hard, jointed EXOSKELETON and paired jointed legs. Includes INSECTS, spiders, crabs, etc.

Baleen horny substance commonly known as whalebone and growing as plates in the mouth of certain whales; used as a fringelike sieve for extracting plankton from seawater

Bill often called the beak: the jaws of a bird, consisting of two bony MANDIBLES, upper and lower, and their horny sheaths

Biodiversity the variety of SPECIES and the variation within them

Biome a major world landscape characterized by having similar plants and animals living in it, e.g., DESERT, jungle, forest

Biped any animal that walks on two legs. See QUADRUPED

Blowhole the nostril opening on the head of a whale through which it breathes

Breeding season the entire cycle of reproductive activity, from courtship, pair formation (and often establishment of territory) through nesting to independence of young

Bristle in birds a modified feather, with a bare or partly bare shaft, like a stiff hair; functions include protection, as with eyelashes of ostriches and hornbills, and touch sensors to help catch INSECTS, as with flycatchers

Brood the young hatching from a single CLUTCH of eggs

Browsing feeding on leaves of trees and shrubs

Cage bird A bird kept in captivity; in this set it usually refers to birds taken from the wild

Canine tooth a sharp stabbing tooth usually longer than the rest

Canopy continuous (closed) or broken (open) layer in forests produced by the intermingling of branches of trees

Carapace the upper part of a shell in a CHELONIAN

Carnivore meat-eating animal

Carrion rotting flesh of dead animals

Casque the raised portion on the head of certain REPTILES and birds

Catadromous fish that spend most of their life in fresh water but MIGRATE to the sea for SPAWNING, e.g., eels

Caudal fin the tail fin in fish

Cephalothorax a body region of CRUSTACEANS formed by the union of the head and THORAX. See PROSOMA

Chelicerae the first pair of appendages ("limbs") on the PROSOMA of spiders, scorpions, etc. Often equipped to inject venom

Chelonian any REPTILE of the ORDER Chelonia, including the tortoises and turtles, in which most of the body is enclosed in a bony capsule

Chrysalis the PUPA in moths and butterflies

Class a large TAXONOMIC group of related animals. MAMMALS, INSECTS, and REPTILES are all CLASSES of animals

Cloaca cavity in the pelvic region into which the alimentary canal, genital, and urinary ducts open

Cloud forest moist, high-altitude forest characterized by a dense UNDERSTORY and an abundance of ferns, mosses, and other plants growing on the trunks and branches of trees

Clutch a set of eggs laid by a female bird in a single breeding attempt

Cocoon the protective coat of many insect LARVAE before they develop into PUPAE or the silken covering secreted to protect the eggs

Colonial living together in a colony

Coniferous forest evergreen forests found in northern regions and mountainous areas, dominated by pines, spruce, and cedars

Costal riblike

Costal grooves grooves running around the body of some TERRESTRIAL salamanders; they conduct water from the ground to the upper parts of the body

Coverts small feathers covering the bases of a bird's main flight feathers on the wings and tail, providing a smooth, streamlined surface for flight

Crustacean member of a CLASS within the PHYLUM Arthropoda typified by five pairs of legs, two pairs of antennae, a joined head and THORAX, and calcerous deposits in the EXOSKELETON; e.g., crabs, shrimps, etc.

Deciduous forest dominated by trees that lose their leaves in winter (or in the dry season)

Deforestation the process of cutting down and removing trees for timber or to create open space for growing crops, grazing animals, etc.

Desert area of low rainfall typically with sparse scrub or grassland vegetation or lacking it altogether

Diatoms microscopic single-celled ALGAE

Dispersal the scattering of young animals going to live away from where they were born and brought up

Diurnal active during the day

DNA (deoxyribonucleic acid) the substance that makes up the main part of the chromosomes of all living things; contains the genetic code that is handed down from generation to generation

Domestication process of taming and breeding animals to provide help and useful products for humans

Dormancy a state in which—as a result of hormone action—growth is suspended and METABOLIC activity is reduced to a minimum

Dorsal relating to the back or spinal part of the body; usually the upper surface

Down soft, fluffy, insulating feathers with few or no shafts found after hatching on young birds and in ADULTS beneath the main feathers

Echolocation the process of perception based on reaction to the pattern of reflected sound waves (echos); occurs in bats

Ecology the study of plants and animals in relation to one another and to their surroundings

Ecosystem a whole system in which plants, animals, and their environment interact

Ectotherm animal that relies on external heat sources to raise body temperature; also known as "cold-blooded"

Edentate toothless; also any animals of the order Edentata, which includes anteaters, sloths, and armadillos

Endemic found only in one geographical area, nowhere else

Epitoke a form of marine ANNELID having particularly well developed swimming appendages

Estivation inactivity or greatly decreased activity during hot weather

Eutrophication an increase in the nutrient chemicals (nitrate, phosphate, etc.) in water, sometimes occurring naturally and sometimes caused by human activities, e.g., by the release of sewage or agricultural fertilizers

Exoskeleton a skeleton covering the outside of the body or situated in the skin, as found in some INVERTEBRATES

Explosive breeding in some AMPHIBIANS when breeding is completed over one or a very few days and nights

Extinction process of dying out at the end of which the very last individual dies, and the SPECIES is lost forever

Family a group of closely related SPECIES that often also look quite similar. Zoological FAMILY names always end in -idae. Also used to describe a social group within a SPECIES comprising parents and their offspring

Feral domestic animals that have gone wild and live independently of people

Flagship species A high-profile SPECIES, which (if present) is likely to be accompanied by many others that are typical of the habitat. (If a naval flagship is present, so is the rest of the fleet of warships and support vessels)

Fledging period the period between a young bird hatching and acquiring its first full set of feathers and being able to fly

Fledgling young bird that is capable of flight; in perching birds and some others it corresponds with the time of leaving the nest

Fluke either of the two lobes of the tail of a whale or related animal; also a type of flatworm, usually parasitic

Gamebird birds in the ORDER Galliformes (megapodes, cracids, grouse, partridges, quail, pheasants, and relatives); also used for any birds that may be legally hunted by humans

Gene the basic unit of heredity, enabling one generation to pass on characteristics to its offspring

Genus (**genera**, pl.) a group of closely related SPECIES

Gestation the period of pregnancy in MAMMALS, between fertilization of the egg and birth of the baby

Gill Respiratory organ that absorbs oxygen from the water. External gills occur in tadpoles. Internal gills occur in most fish

Harem a group of females living in the same territory and consorting with a single male

Hen any female bird

Herbivore an animal that eats plants (grazers and BROWSERS are herbivores)

Hermaphrodite an animal having both male and female reproductive organs

Herpetologist ZOOLOGIST who studies REPTILES and AMPHIBIANS

Hibernation becoming inactive in winter, with lowered body temperature to save energy. Hibernation takes place in a special nest or den called a hibernaculum

Homeotherm an animal that can maintain a high and constant body temperature by means of internal processes; also called "warm-blooded"

Home range the area that an animal uses in the course of its normal activity

Hybrid offspring of two closely related SPECIES that can breed; it is sterile and so cannot produce offspring

Ichthyologist ZOOLOGIST specializing in the study of fish

Inbreeding breeding among closely related animals (e.g., cousins), leading to weakened genetic composition and reduced survival rates

Incubation the act of keeping the egg or eggs warm or the period from the laying of eggs to hatching

Indwellers ORGANISMS that live inside others, e.g., the California Bay pea crab, which lives in the tubes of some marine ANNELID worms, but do not act as PARASITES

Indigenous living naturally in a region; native (i.e., not an introduced SPECIES)

Insect any air-breathing ARTHROPOD of the CLASS Insecta, having a body divided into head, THORAX, and abdomen, three pairs of legs, and sometimes two pairs of wings

Insectivore animal that feeds on INSECTS. Also used as a group name for hedgehogs, shrews, moles, etc.

Interbreeding breeding between animals of different SPECIES, varieties, etc. within a single FAMILY or strain; Interbreeding can cause dilution of the GENE pool

Interspecific between SPECIES

Intraspecific between individuals of the same SPECIES

Invertebrates animals that have no backbone (or other bones) inside their body, e.g., mollusks, INSECTS, jellyfish, crabs

Iridescent displaying glossy colors produced (e.g., in bird PLUMAGE) not as a result of pigments but by the splitting of sunlight into light of different wavelengths; rainbows are made in the same way

Joey a young kangaroo living in its mother's pouch

Juvenile a young animal that has not yet reached breeding age

Keel a ridge along the CARAPACE of certain turtles or a ridge on the scales of some REPTILES

Keratin tough, fibrous material that forms hair, feathers, nails, and protective plates on the skin of VERTEBRATE animals

Keystone species a SPECIES on which many other SPECIES are wholly or partially dependent

Krill PLANKTONIC shrimps

Labyrinth specialized auxiliary (extra) breathing organ found in some fish

Larva an immature form of an animal that develops into an ADULT form through METAMORPHOSIS

Lateral line system a system of pores running along a fish's body. These pores lead to nerve endings that allow a fish to sense vibrations in the water and help it locate prey, detect PREDATORS, avoid obstacles, and so on. Also found in AMPHIBIANS

Lek communal display area where male birds of some SPECIES gather to attract and mate with females

Livebearer animal that gives birth to fully developed young (usually refers to REPTILES or fish)

Mammal any animal of the CLASS Mammalia—warm-blooded VERTEBRATE having mammary glands in the female that produce milk with which it nurses its young. The class includes bats, primates, rodents, and whales

Mandible upper or lower part of a bird's beak or BILL; also the jawbone in VERTEBRATES; in INSECTS and other ARTHROPODS mandibles are mouth parts mostly used for biting and chewing

Mantle cavity a space in the body of mollusks that contains the breathing organs

Marine living in the sea

Matriarch senior female member of a social group

Metabolic rate the rate at which chemical activities occur within animals, including the exchange of gasses in respiration and the liberation of energy from food

Metamorphosis the transformation of a LARVA into an ADULT

Migration movement from one place to another and back again; usually seasonal

Molt the process in which a bird sheds its feathers and replaces them with new ones; some MAMMALS, REPTILES, and ARTHROPODS regularly molt, shedding hair, skin, or outer layers

Monotreme egg-laying MAMMAL, e.g., platypus

Montane in a mountain environment

Natural selection the process whereby individuals with the most appropriate ADAPTATIONS are more successful than other individuals and therefore survive to produce more offspring. Natural selection is the main process driving evolution in which animals and plants are challenged by natural effects (such as predation and bad weather), resulting in survival of the fittest

Nematocyst the stinging part of animals such as jellyfish, usually found on the tentacles

Nestling a young bird still in the nest and dependent on its parents

New World the Americas

Niche part of a habitat occupied by an ORGANISM, defined in terms of all aspects of its lifestyle

Nocturnal active at night

Nomadic animals that have no fixed home, but wander continuously

Noseleaf fleshy structures around the face of bats; helps focus ULTRASOUNDS used for ECHOLOCATION

Ocelli markings on an animal's body that resemble eyes. Also, the tiny, simple eyes of some INSECTS, spiders, CRUSTACEANS, mollusks, etc.

Old World non-American continents

Olfaction sense of smell

Operculum a cover consisting of bony plates that covers the GILLS of fish

Omnivore an animal that eats a wide range of both animal and vegetable food

Order a subdivision of a CLASS of animals, consisting of a series of animal FAMILIES

Organism any member of the animal or plant kingdom; a body that has life

Ornithologist ZOOLOGIST specializing in the study of birds

Osteoderms bony plates beneath the scales of some REPTILES, particularly crocodilians

Oviparous producing eggs that hatch outside the body of the mother (in fish, REPTILES, birds, and MONOTREMES)

Parasite an animal or plant that lives on or within the body of another (the host) from which it obtains nourishment. The host is often harmed by the association

Passerine any bird of the ORDER Passeriformes; includes SONGBIRDS

Pedipalps small, paired leglike appendages immediately in front of the first pair of walking legs of spiders and other ARACHNIDS. Used by males for transferring sperm to the females

Pelagic living in the upper waters of the open sea or large lakes

Pheromone scent produced by animals to enable others to find and recognize them

Photosynthesis the production of food in green plants using sunlight as an energy source and water plus carbon dioxide as raw materials

Phylum zoological term for a major grouping of animal CLASSES. The whole animal kingdom is divided into about 30 PHYLA, of which the VERTEBRATES form part of just one

Placenta the structure that links an embryo to its mother during pregnancy, allowing exchange of chemicals between them

Plankton animals and plants drifting in open water; many are minute

Plastron the lower shell of CHELONIANS

Plumage the covering of feathers on a bird's body

Plume a long feather used for display, as in a bird of paradise

Polygamous where an individual has more than one mate in one BREEDING SEASON. Monogamous animals have only a single mate

Polygynous where a male mates with several females in one BREEDING SEASON

Polyp individual ORGANISM that lives as part of a COLONY—e.g., a coral—with a saclike body opening only by the mouth that is usually surrounded by a ring of tentacles

Population a distinct group of animals of the same SPECIES or all the animals of that SPECIES

Posterior the hind end or behind another structure

Predator an animal that kills live prey

Prehensile capable of grasping

Primary forest forest that has always been forest and has not been cut down and regrown at some time

Primates a group of MAMMALS that includes monkeys, apes, and ourselves

Prosoma the joined head and THORAX of a spider, scorpion, or horseshoe crab

Pupa an INSECT in the stage of METAMORPHOSIS between a caterpillar (LARVA) and an ADULT (imago)

Quadruped any animal that walks on four legs

Range the total geographical area over which a SPECIES is distributed

Raptor bird with hooked beak and strong feet with sharp claws (talons) for seizing, killing, and dealing with prey; also known as birds of prey. The term usually refers to daytime birds of prey (eagles, hawks, falcons, and relatives) but sometimes also includes NOCTURNAL owls

Regurgitate (of a bird) to vomit partly digested food either to feed NESTLINGS or to rid itself of bones, fur, or other indigestible parts, or (in some seabirds) to scare off PREDATORS

Reptile any member of the cold-blooded CLASS Reptilia, such as crocodiles, lizards, snakes, tortoises, turtles, and tuataras; characterized by an external covering of scales or horny plates. Most are egg-layers, but some give birth to fully developed young

Roost place that a bird or bat regularly uses for sleeping

Ruminant animals that eat vegetation and later bring it back from the stomach to chew again ("chewing the cud") to assist its digestion by microbes in the stomach

Savanna open grasslands with scattered trees and low rainfall, usually in warm areas

Scapulars the feathers of a bird above its shoulders

Scent chemicals produced by animals to leave smell messages for others to find and interpret

Scrub vegetation dominated by shrubs—woody plants usually with more than one stem

Scute horny plate covering live body tissue underneath

Secondary forest trees that have been planted or grown up on cleared ground

Sedge grasslike plant

Shorebird Plovers, sandpipers, and relatives (known as waders in Britain, Australia, and some other areas)

Slash-and-burn agriculture method of farming in which the unwanted vegetation is cleared by cutting down and burning

Social behavior interactions between individuals within the same SPECIES, e.g., courtship

Songbird member of major bird group of PASSERINES

Spawning the laying and fertilizing of eggs by fish and AMPHIBIANS and some mollusks

Speciation the origin of SPECIES; the diverging of two similar ORGANISMS

through reproduction down through the generations into different forms resulting in a new SPECIES

Species a group of animals that look similar and can breed with each other to produce fertile offspring

Steppe open grassland in parts of the world where the climate is too harsh for trees to grow

Subspecies a subpopulation of a single SPECIES whose members are similar to each other but differ from the typical form for that SPECIES; often called a race

Substrate a medium to which fixed animals are attached under water, such as rocks onto which barnacles and mussels are attached, or plants are anchored in, e.g., gravel, mud, or sand in which AQUATIC plants have their roots embedded

Substratum see SUBSTRATE

Swim bladder a gas or air-filled bladder in fish; by taking in or exhaling air, the fish can alter its buoyancy

Symbiosis a close relationship between members of two SPECIES from which both partners benefit

Taxonomy the branch of biology concerned with classifying ORGANISMS into groups according to similarities in their structure, origins, or behavior. The categories, in order of increasing broadness, are: SPECIES, GENUS, FAMILY, ORDER, CLASS, PHYLUM

Terrestrial living on land

Territory defended space

Test an external covering or "shell" of an INVERTEBRATE such as a sea-urchin; it is in fact an internal skeleton just below the skin

Thorax (**thoracic**, adj.) in an INSECT the middle region of the body between the head and the abdomen. It bears the wings and three pairs of walking legs

Torpor deep sleep accompanied by lowered body temperature and reduced METABOLIC RATE

Translocation transferring members of a SPECIES from one location to another

Tundra open grassy or shrub-covered lands of the far north

Underfur fine hairs forming a dense, woolly mass close to the skin and underneath the outer coat of stiff hairs in MAMMALS

Understory the layer of shrubs,

herbs, and small trees found beneath the forest CANOPY

Ungulate one of a large group of hoofed animals such as pigs, deer, cattle, and horses; mostly HERBIVORES

Uterus womb in which embryos of MAMMALS develop

Ultrasounds sounds that are too high-pitched for humans to hear

UV-B radiation component of ultraviolet radiation from the sun that is harmful to living ORGANISMS because it breaks up DNA

Vane the bladelike main part of a typical bird feather extending from either side of its shaft (midrib)

Ventral of or relating to the front part or belly of an animal (see DORSAL)

Vertebrate animal with a backbone (e.g., fish, MAMMAL, REPTILE), usually with skeleton made of bones, but sometimes softer cartilage

Vestigial a characteristic with little or no use, but derived from one that was well developed in an ancestral form; e.g., the "parson's nose" (the fatty end portion of the tail when a fowl is cooked) is the compressed bones from the long tail of the reptilian ancestor of birds

Viviparous (of most MAMMALS and a few other VERTEBRATES) giving birth to active young rather than laying eggs

Waterfowl members of the bird FAMILY Anatidae, the swans, geese, and ducks; sometimes used to include other groups of wild AQUATIC birds

Wattle fleshy protuberance, usually near the base of a bird's BILL

Wingbar line of contrasting feathers on a bird's wing

Wing case one of the protective structures formed from the first pair of nonfunctional wings, which are used to protect the second pair of functional wings in INSECTS such as beetles

Wintering ground the area where a migrant spends time outside the BREEDING SEASON

Yolk part of the egg that contains nourishment for a growing embryo

Zooid individual animal in a colony; usually applied to corals or bryozoa (sea-mats)

Zoologist person who studies animals

Zoology the study of animals

Further Reading

Mammals

Macdonald, David, *The Encyclopedia of Mammals*, Barnes & Noble, New York, U.S., 2001

Payne, Roger, *Among Whales*, Bantam Press, U.S., 1996

Reeves, R. R., and Leatherwood, S., *The Sierra Club Handbook of Whales and Dolphins of the World*, Sierra Club, U.S., 1983

Sherrow, Victoria, and Cohen, Sandee, *Endangered Mammals of North America*, Twenty-First Century Books, U.S., 1995

Whitaker, J. O., *Audubon Society Field Guide to North American Mammals*, Alfred A. Knopf, New York, U.S., 1996

Birds

Attenborough, David, *The Life of Birds*, BBC Books, London, U.K., 1998

BirdLife International, *Threatened Birds of the World*, Lynx Edicions, Barcelona, Spain and BirdLife International, Cambridge, U.K., 2000

del Hoyo, J., Elliott, A., and Sargatal, J., eds., *Handbook of Birds of the World* Vols 1 to 6, Lynx Edicions, Barcelona, Spain, 1992–2001

Sayre, April Pulley, *Endangered Birds of North America*, Scientific American Sourcebooks, Twenty-First Century Books, U.S., 1977

Scott, Shirley L., ed., *A Field Guide to the Birds of North America*, National Geographic, U.S., 1999

Stattersfield, A., Crosby, M., Long, A., and Wege, D., eds., *Endemic Bird Areas of the World: Priorities for Biodiversity Conservation*, BirdLife International, Cambridge, U.K., 1998

Thomas, Peggy, *Bird Alert: Science of Saving*, Twenty-First Century Books, U.S., 2000

Fish

Bannister, Keith, and Campbell, Andrew, *The Encyclopedia of Aquatic Life*, Facts On File, New York, U.S., 1997

Buttfield, Helen, *The Secret Lives of Fishes*, Abrams, U.S., 2000

Reptiles and Amphibians

Corbett, Keith, *Conservation of European Reptiles and Amphibians*, Christopher Helm, London, U.K., 1989

Corton, Misty, *Leopard and Other South African Tortoises*, Carapace Press, London, U.K., 2000

Hofrichter, Robert, *Amphibians: The World of Frogs, Toads, Salamanders, and Newts*, Firefly Books, Canada, 2000

Stafford, Peter, *Snakes*, Natural History Museum, London, U.K., 2000

Insects

Borror, Donald J., and White, Richard E., *A Field Guide to Insects: America, North of Mexico*, Houghton Mifflin, New York, U.S., 1970

Pyle, Robert Michael, *National Audubon Society Field Guide to North American Butterflies*, Alfred A. Knopf, New York, U.S., 1995

General

Adams, Douglas, and Carwardine, Mark, *Last Chance to See*, Random House, London, U.K., 1992

Allaby, Michael, *The Concise Oxford Dictionary of Ecology*, Oxford University Press, Oxford, U.K., 1998

Douglas, Dougal, and others, *Atlas of Life on Earth*, Barnes & Noble, New York, U.S., 2001

National Wildlife Federation, *Endangered Species: Wild and Rare*, McGraw-Hill, U.S., 1996

Websites

http://www.abcbirds.org/ American Bird Conservancy. Articles, information about campaigns and bird conservation in the Americas

http://elib.cs.berkeley.edu/aw/ AmphibiaWeb information about amphibians and their conservation

http://animaldiversity.ummz.umich.edu/ University of Michigan Museum of Zoology animal diversity web. Search for pictures and information about animals by class, family, and common name. Includes glossary

www.beachside.org sea turtle preservation society

http://www.birdlife.net BirdLife International, an alliance of conservation organizations working in more than 100 countries to save birds and their habitats

http://www.surfbirds.com Articles, mystery photographs, news, book reviews, birding polls, and more

http://www.birds.cornell.edu/ Cornell University. Courses, news, nest-box cam

http://www.cites.org/ CITES and IUCN listings. Search for animals by scientific name of order, family, genus, species, or common name. Location by country and explanation of reasons for listings

www.ufl.edu/natsci/herpetology/ crocs.htm crocodile site, including a chat room

www.darwinfoundation.org/ Charles Darwin Research Center

http://www.open.cc.uk/daptf DAPTF–Decllining Amphibian Population Task Force. Providing information and data about amphibian declines. (International Director, Professor Tim Halliday, is co-author of this set)

http://www.ucmp.berkeley.edu/ echinodermata the echinoderm phylum—starfish, sea-urchins, etc.

http://endangered.fws.gov information about endangered animals and plants from the U.S. Fish and Wildlife Service, the organization in charge of 94 million acres of wildlife refuges

http://forests.org/ includes forest conservation answers to queries

www.traffic.org/turtles freshwater turtles

www.iucn.org details of species, IUCN listings and IUCN publications

http://www.pbs.org/journeytoamazonia the Amazonian rain forest and its unrivaled biodiversity

http://www.audubon.org National Audubon Society, named after the ornithologist and wildlife artist John James Audubon (1785–1851). Sections on education, local Audubon societies, and bird identification

www.nccnsw.org.au site for threatened Australian species

http://cmc-ocean.org facts, figures, and quizzes about marine life

http://wwwl.nature.nps.gov/wv/ The U.S. National Park Service wildlife and plants site. Factsheets on all kinds of animals found in the parks

www.ewt.org.za endangered South African wildlife

http://www.panda.org World Wide Fund for Nature (WWF). Newsroom, press releases, government reports, campaigns. Themed photogallery

http://www.greenchannel.com/wwt/ Wildfowl and Wetlands Trust (U.K.). Founded by artist and naturalist Sir Peter Scott, the trust aims to preserve wetlands for rare waterbirds. Includes information on places to visit and threatened waterbird species

http://wdcs.org/ Whale and Dolphin Conservation Society site. News, projects, and campaigns. Sightings database

List of Animals by Group

Listed below are the common names of the animals featured in the A–Z part of this set grouped by their class, i.e., Mammals, Birds, Fish, Reptiles, Amphibians, and Insects and Invertebrates.

Bold numbers indicate the volume number and are followed by the first page number of the two-page illustrated main entry in the set.

Mammals

addax **2**:4
anoa, mountain **2**:20
anteater, giant **2**:24
antelope, Tibetan **2**:26
armadillo, giant **2**:30
ass
  African wild **2**:34
  Asiatic wild **2**:36
aye-aye **2**:42
babirusa **2**:44
baboon, gelada **2**:46
bandicoot, western barred **2**:48
banteng **2**:50
bat
  ghost **2**:56
  gray **2**:58
  greater horseshoe **2**:60
  greater mouse-eared **2**:62
  Kitti's hog-nosed **2**:64
  Morris's **2**:66
bear
  grizzly **2**:68
  polar **2**:70
  sloth **2**:72
  spectacled **2**:74
beaver, Eurasian **2**:76
bison
  American **2**:86
  European **2**:88
blackbuck **2**:94
camel, wild bactrian **3**:24
cat, Iriomote **3**:30
cheetah **3**:40
chimpanzee **3**:42
  pygmy **3**:44
chinchilla, short-tailed **3**:46
cow, Steller's sea **3**:70
cuscus, black-spotted **3**:86
deer
  Chinese water **4**:6
  Kuhl's **4**:8
  Père David's **4**:10
  Siberian musk **4**:12
desman, Russian **4**:14
dhole **4**:16
dog
  African wild **4**:22

bush **4**:24
dolphin
  Amazon river **4**:26
  Yangtze river **4**:28
dormouse
  common **4**:30
  garden **4**:32
  Japanese **4**:34
drill **4**:40
dugong **4**:46
duiker, Jentink's **4**:48
dunnart, Kangaroo Island **4**:50
echidna, long-beaked **4**:60
elephant
  African **4**:64
  Asian **4**:66
elephant-shrew, golden-rumped **4**:68
ferret, black-footed **4**:72
flying fox
  Rodrigues (Rodriguez) **4**:84
  Ryukyu **4**:86
fossa **4**:90
fox, swift **4**:92
gaur **5**:18
gazelle, dama **5**:20
gibbon, black **5**:26
giraffe, reticulated **5**:30
glider, mahogany **5**:32
gorilla
  mountain **5**:38
  western lowland **5**:40
gymnure, Hainan **5**:48
hare, hispid **5**:50
hippopotamus, pygmy **5**:52
horse, Przewalski's wild **5**:58
hutia, Jamaican **5**:64
hyena
  brown **5**:66
  spotted **5**:68
ibex, Nubian **5**:70
indri **5**:84
jaguar **5**:86
koala **6**:10
kouprey **6**:14
kudu, greater **6**:16
lemur
  hairy-eared dwarf **6**:22
  Philippine flying **6**:24
  ruffed **6**:26
leopard **6**:28
  clouded **6**:30
  snow **6**:32
lion, Asiatic **6**:34
loris, slender **6**:46
lynx, Iberian **6**:52
macaque
  barbary **6**:54
  Japanese **6**:56
manatee, Florida **6**:68
markhor **6**:72
marten, pine **6**:74
mink, European **6**:78

mole, marsupial **6**:80
mole-rat
  Balkans **6**:82
  giant **6**:84
monkey
  douc **6**:86
  Goeldi's **6**:88
  proboscis **6**:90
mouse, St. Kilda **6**:92
mulgara **6**:94
numbat **7**:14
nyala, mountain **7**:18
ocelot, Texas **7**:20
okapi **7**:22
orang-utan **7**:26
oryx
  Arabian **7**:28
  scimitar-horned **7**:30
otter
  European **7**:32
  giant **7**:34
  sea **7**:36
ox, Vu Quang **7**:44
panda
  giant **7**:48
  lesser **7**:50
pangolin, long-tailed **7**:52
panther, Florida **7**:54
pig, Visayan warty **7**:68
pika, steppe **7**:74
platypus **7**:82
porpoise, harbor **7**:86
possum, Leadbeater's **7**:88
potoroo, long-footed **7**:90
prairie dog, black-tailed **7**:92
pygmy-possum, mountain **8**:4
quagga **8**:8
rabbit
  Amami **8**:12
  volcano **8**:14
rat, black **8**:24
rhinoceros
  black **8**:26
  great Indian **8**:28
  Javan **8**:30
  Sumatran **8**:32
  white **8**:34
rock-wallaby, Prosperine **8**:36
saiga **8**:42
sea lion, Steller's **8**:62
seal
  Baikal **8**:70
  gray **8**:72
  Hawaiian monk **8**:74
  Mediterranean monk **8**:76
  northern fur **8**:78
sheep, barbary **8**:88
shrew, giant otter **8**:90
sifaka, golden-crowned **8**:92
sloth, maned **9**:6
solenodon, Cuban **9**:16
souslik, European **9**:18
squirrel, Eurasian red **9**:28

tahr, Nilgiri **9**:46
takin **9**:50
tamarin, golden lion **9**:52
tapir
  Central American **9**:56
  Malayan **9**:58
tenrec, aquatic **9**:64
thylacine **9**:66
tiger **9**:68
tree-kangaroo, Goodfellow's **10**:4
vicuña **10**:28
whale
  blue **10**:40
  fin **10**:42
  gray **10**:44
  humpback **10**:46
  killer **10**:48
  minke **10**:50
  northern right **10**:52
  sei **10**:54
  sperm **10**:56
  white **10**:58
wildcat **10**:62
wolf
  Ethiopian **10**:64
  Falkland Island **10**:66
  gray **10**:68
  maned **10**:70
  red **10**:72
wolverine **10**:74
wombat, northern hairy-nosed **10**:76
yak, wild **10**:90
zebra
  Grevy's **10**:92
  mountain **10**:94

Birds

akiapolaau **2**:6
albatross, wandering **2**:8
amazon, St. Vincent **2**:14
asity, yellow-bellied **2**:32
auk, great **2**:38
barbet, toucan **2**:54
bellbird, three-wattled **2**:82
bird of paradise, blue **2**:84
bittern, Eurasian **2**:90
blackbird, saffron-cowled **2**:92
bowerbird, Archbold's **3**:8
bustard, great **3**:10
cassowary, southern **3**:28
cockatoo, salmon-crested **3**:52
condor, California **3**:60
coot, horned **3**:62
cormorant, Galápagos **3**:64
corncrake **3**:66
courser, Jerdon's **3**:68
crane, whooping **3**:76
crow, Hawaiian **3**:82
curlew, Eskimo **3**:84
dipper, rufous-throated **4**:18

Set Index

Acknowledgments

The authors and publishers would like to thank the following people and organizations:
Aquamarines International Pvt. Ltd., Sri Lanka, especially Ananda Pathirana; Aquarist & Pond keeper Magazine, U.K.; BirdLife International (the global partnership of conservation organizations working together in over 100 countries to save birds and their habitats). Special thanks to David Capper; also to Guy Dutson and Alison Stattersfield; Sylvia Clarke (Threatened Wildlife, South Australia); Mark Cocker (writer and birder); David Curran (aquarist specializing in spiny eels, U.K.); Marydele Donnelly (IUCN sea turtle specialist); Svein Fossa (aquatic consultant, Norway); Richard Gibson (Jersey Wildlife Preservation Trust, Channel Islands); Paul Hoskisson (Liverpool John Moores University); Derek Lambert; Pat Lambert (aquarists specializing in freshwater livebearers); Lumbini Aquaria Wayamba Ltd., Sri Lanka, especially Jayantha Ramasinghe and Vibhu Perera; Isolda McGeorge (Chester Zoological Gardens); Dr. James Peron Ross (IUCN crocodile specialist); Zoological Society of London, especially Michael Palmer, Ann Sylph, and the other library staff.

Picture Credits

Abbreviations

AL   Ardea London
BBC   BBC Natural History Unit
BCC   Bruce Coleman Collection
FLPA   Frank Lane Photographic Agency
NHPA   Natural History Photographic Agency
OSF   Oxford Scientific Films
PEP   Planet Earth Pictures
b = bottom; **c** = center; **t** = top; **l** = left; **r** = right

Jacket

Ibiza wall lizard, illustration by Denys Ovenden from *Collins Field Guide: Reptiles and Amphibians of Britain and Europe*; Grevy's zebra, Stan Osolinski/Oxford Scientific Films; Florida panther, Lynn M. Stone/BBC Natural History Unit; silver shark, Max Gibbs/Photomax; blue whale, Tui de Roy/Oxford Scientific Films

4–5 Animals Animals/Zig Leszczynski/OSF; **6–7** Michael Leach/OSF; **11** Franz Bagyi/BCC; **13** E.J. & J.S. Woolmer/OSF; **17** C.B. & D.W. Frith/BCC; **17** inset Alain Compost/BCC; **20–21** & **21** Alastair Shay/OSF; **23** John Woolmer/OSF; **24–25** Colin Monteath/OSF; **29** Tom Leach/OSF; **31** Makoto Yokotsuka/Nature Production; **35** Joe Tomelleri; **37c** & **37b** Robert & Valerie Davies; **39** Max Gibbs/Photomax; **39** inset Ken Lucas/PEP; **40–41** Hilary Pooley/OSF; **41** Daniel J. Cox/OSF; **42–43** Clive Bromhall/OSF; **45** Martyn Colbeck/OSF; **49t** & **49c** Max Gibbs/Photomax; **51** David B. Fleetham/OSF; **55** Fredrik Ehrenstrom/OSF; **59** Peter Scoones/PEP; **61** Animals Animals/Dr. Mark A. Chappell/OSF; **62–63** Barry Wright/Windrush Photos; **65** Dr. Eckart Pott/BCC; **66–67** Alan Williams/NHPA; **73** Jane Burton/BCC; **74–75** Animals Animals/Breck P. Kent/OSF; **77** Ken Lucas/PEP; **79** Daniel Heuclin/NHPA; **80–81** Bob Bennett/OSF; **83** Paul Banko/BirdLife International; **85** BCC; **87** Philip Chapman/PEP; **89** & **89** inset Robin Crump; **91** Richard Biggins/U.S. Fish & Wildlife Service; **93** K.G. Preston-Mafham/Premaphotos Wildlife; **95** W. Tomey.

Artists

Graham Allen, Norman Arlott, Priscilla Barrett, Trevor Boyer, Ad Cameron, David Dennis, Karen Hiscock, Chloe Talbot Kelly, Mick Loates, Michael Long, Malcolm McGregor, Denys Ovenden, Oxford Illustrators, John Sibbick, Joseph Tomelleri, Dick Twinney, Ian Willis